Praise
Breaking Big Money's Grip

"A brilliant analysis of where we are and where we need to go. Read this book!"

—Thom Hartmann
Author and talk radio show host

"This book persuasively argues that the dominance of Big Money not only corrupts government itself but also blocks effective action on virtually every major issue Americans care about. As Bruce Berlin makes clear, and our history confirms, the only force capable of challenging Big Money's corrupt and powerful hegemony is a diverse, nonpartisan, grassroots movement for democracy based on a politics of human dignity and equality. Such a movement is needed now more than ever. Fortunately, Berlin lays out a credible roadmap showing how we can create it. I hope it's read by millions."

—Randy Kehler
Former national coordinator,
Nuclear Weapons Freeze Campaign

"In this highly readable, compelling analysis of America's current political crises, Bruce Berlin calls for a second American revolution to be carried out by the organization of a massive Democracy Movement. He advocates taking on the corruptions of self government visited upon us by almost unlimited corporate campaign contributions, billions of corporate dollars spent lobbying Congress and the states, and dilution of the rule of law in our courts, all of which must be contested if democracy is to survive."

—Craig Barnes
Award-winning author and member of
Common Cause National Board

"In this small but profoundly important book, Bruce Berlin tells us everything we need to know to incite inspired and organized rebellion against Big Money's hijacking of our democracy. In example after example, he shows how corporate America is choosing how we will live. If you don't read another book this year, read this one. Berlin reveals the stark reality that the United States is, by and large, a government of, by, and for corporations."

—Gail Carr Feldman, PhD
Psychologist and author

"I highly recommend this very insightful book about what is wrong with our political system and how to fix it. Everyone, especially young people who are dismayed with our politics, needs to read it. Whether you are a Republican, Democrat, or Independent, Berlin's proposals can work for all of us."

—David Cortez
Community organizer and filmmaker, Taos, New Mexico

"The crippling influence of money in our political system has undermined the solid science and soulful connections that have long been pressing for fundamental changes in our relationship with all of life. This book is a much-needed clarion call that we must take to heart."

—Jim Cummings
Executive director, Acoustic Ecology Institute

"Big corporate money greatly inflates what we pay for medical care and prescription drugs. That's why profits are the only vital signs in our fragmented healthcare system. Berlin's book breaks it all down to the personal level, where your life and mine are manipulated by Big Money. He astutely illustrates why the grassroots level offers us the best chance to break Big Money's grip."

—Al Norman
Executive director, Massachusetts Home Care Association

"Berlin is issuing a compelling clarion call to all who are fed up with Big Money."

—Charlotte Levinson
President, The Levinson Foundation

"For many years I have watched Big Money over-influencing our representative democracy. Bruce Berlin's six-point plan is right on target, giving us a way forward and a path back to sanity."

—Richard Schmeltzer, CPA
Retired Partner Philadelphia region CPA firm

"With insight and riveting clarity, Bruce Berlin examines how today's Big Money–powered plutocracy has grown in this country and then counters with a doable plan for the American people to build a bridge back to a democracy."

—Eric von Starck
Small business owner

BREAKING BIG MONEY'S GRIP ON AMERICA

WORKING TOGETHER
TO REVIVE OUR DEMOCRACY

BRUCE BERLIN

OUR TIME BOOKS

Santa Fe, New Mexico

Published by: Our Time Books
2840 Vereda de Pueblo
Santa Fe, NM 87507
www.breakingbigmoneysgrip.com

Editors: Carole Tashel, Ellen Kleiner, and Ann Mason
Book design and production: Janice St. Marie
Cover art and logo: Warren Godfrey

First Edition

Printed in the United States of America

Publisher's Cataloging-in-Publication Data

Berlin, Bruce M.

Breaking big money's grip on America : working together to revive our democracy / Bruce Berlin. -- First edition. -- Santa Fe, New Mexico : Our Time Books, [2016]

pages ; cm.

ISBN: 978-0-9966232-0-9 (pbk.) ; 978-0-9966232-1-6 (ebook)
Includes bibliographical references.
Summary: A wake-up call to the people of the United States. The book addresses the problem of the broken political system caused by the dominance of Big Money and corporate America, and examines what the American people can do to build a government that works for everyone. It makes the case for why a mass movement involving a broad alliance of people and civic organizations from across the political spectrum is urgently needed to save the United States from becoming a plutocracy, a country run by and for the benefit of the very wealthy.--Publisher.

1. United States--Politics and government--21st century. 2. Legislators--United States--Elections--Finance. 3. Campaign funds-- United States. 4. Political campaigns--United States--Economic aspects. 5. Lobbying--United States. 6. Corporate power--United States. 7. Social movements--United States. 8. Democracy--United States. 9. Political culture--United States. 10. Elite (Social sciences)-- United States--Political aspects. 11. United States. Congress--Reform. 12. Income distribution--United States--Political aspects. I. Title.

JK275 .B47 2016   2015913959
320.937/0905--dc23   1602

To my dad, Harold Berlin,
who has been a wonderful role model
throughout my life,
and to my mom, Dorothy Berlin,
who was my generous supporter
throughout her life.

Acknowledgments

This book is the culmination of many years of working in a variety of ways to improve life in America. I received a great deal of help along the way. Mrs. Romero, my high school American history teacher in Camden, New Jersey, first instilled in me the curiosity to examine issues like the ones addressed in this book. At Cornell University, Professors Andrew Hacker, George Kahin, Walter LaFeber, and Clinton Rossiter deepened my concern for how our country is governed. At New York University School of Law, Professor Irving Younger stimulated a strong desire to pursue justice in my work. A few years after graduating from law school, I had the good fortune to study Tibetan Buddhism with Lama Thubten Yeshe and Lama Thubten Zopa Rinpoche at Kopan Monastery in Nepal; some years later I became a student of Zen meditation under Joshu Sasaki Roshi. I will be forever indebted to them for their teachings and guidance.

Through the years many friends and colleagues have inspired and supported my peace and justice work, including Theo Brown, Herb Cohen, Steve Koehler, Leslie LaKind, Meryl Lefkoff, Charlotte Lowrey, Don McAvinchey, Cindy and John McLeod, Craig Schindler, and Robert Spitz. Friends and colleagues who reviewed *Breaking Big Money's Grip on America* and provided invaluable feedback are Margaret Lubalin, Joe Odermatt, Bill O'Hanlon, Gershon Siegel, and Caroline Wareham. I am also grateful for the moral support I received from my daughter, Gioia Berlin, as well as from Annie Chew, Kareena Hamilton, Leonora Lorenzo, and Bobbe Schmeltzer. In addition, I want to thank the Blessingway/PenPower team of Ellen Kleiner, Judy Herzl, and Jeanie C. Williams for all their expert publishing and marketing assistance, and Janice St. Marie for her design excellence; Warren Godfrey deserves special thanks for his brilliant cover design. And finally, I owe my deepest gratitude to my editors Carole Tashel, Ellen Kleiner, and Ann Mason for their insightful and tireless work, without which I would never have completed this project.

CONTENTS

Introduction

What is Big Money? It is the power of vast
sums of money to influence the outcome of elections
and the formation of public policy to favor special interests.

Breaking Big Money's Grip on America is a wake-up call to the people of the United States. Deep inside, many of us believe that we, the people, deserve more than a government that disregards us, media that misinform us, and huge corporations that profit off of us. We see the corruption, greed, ignorance, and self-interest that are poisoning our nation, destroying our environment, eliminating our jobs, devaluing our work, foreclosing on our homes, and killing our youth in needless wars. And we feel powerless, overwhelmed, or unfit to tackle such huge issues.

We are also aware of the ever-growing influence of Big Money on our political system and how it controls governmental policy at the expense of most Americans. Due to Big Money, the needs and desires of the great majority of us are not well represented by our government officials, unlike what we would expect in a truly democratic society. Nevertheless, while many people get involved in public issues or social improvement programs to help better our country in one way or another, most Americans go about their separate lives either unaware of Big Money's harmful influence over our nation or believing they can do little or nothing about it.

Like a great many Americans, I feel that I have very little, if any, say in what policies our federal government adopts, how those policies are implemented, or what impact they may have on my community or on me. This hit home for me especially in 2008 when the Great Recession depressed the US housing market, affecting the value of a residential rental property I had owned since 2000. My plan had been to build equity in my rental unit as an education fund for my young daughter's future college expenses. Just before the Great Recession my rental property had been valued at roughly $300,000 and I had about $100,000 in equity in it. I believed that by the time my daughter, then an eighth grader, entered college her mother and I would be in pretty good shape to afford her college expenses by selling the rental property. However, in the fall of 2008 my plan disintegrated practically overnight when the value of my rental property tanked and I lost all the equity that had built up over the previous eight years. Misguided government policies, combined with unregulated and unscrupulous mortgage and banking practices, had rendered my daughter's college fund bankrupt. An innocent victim, I was angry and disillusioned. I could only imagine how the millions of Americans who had lost their homes or jobs felt.

In fact, millions of lives were shattered. Whether a person had been earning minimum wage or a middle-class salary, it became difficult to make ends met. Many people had their health insurance canceled or their cars repossessed for failing to keep up with their monthly payments, while countless others lost their incomes altogether. Although those working in construction or manufacturing suffered the greatest hardship, almost everyone except the economic elite felt some loss. My outrage only increased when our government not only failed to come to the aid of average Americans who had been hit hard by the financial crisis, but instead bailed out the big Wall Street banks that had been, in large part, responsible for the economic mess the country was in.

Then in November 2008 Barack Obama was elected president. Since he had promised "change we can believe in" during his campaign, I thought there would be no more sweetheart deals for corporate giants similar to the one the too-big-to-fail banks had received from the George W. Bush administration. But I was wrong. First, the Obama administration failed to hold the bankers and mortgage lenders accountable for the fraudulent practices that had been largely responsible for the collapse of the housing market. Then President Obama negotiated a watered-down healthcare bill with the insurance industry and pharmaceutical giants, the Pharmaceutical Research and Manufacturers of America (PhRMA), which met their needs more than those of the American people. To me and many other Americans who had believed in Obama's campaign, he had become just another politician who allowed corporate sponsors to steer the ship of state.

Looking at my experiences during the Great Recession in a larger context, I realize that as a lifelong political activist and student of American government and history I have periodically been dismayed and, at times, even outraged by our nation's increasingly antidemocratic political process. In fact, at one point I felt so disheartened that I considered moving to Costa Rica, Panama, or some peaceful tropical island. But upon further reflection I saw that such an easy escape would not contribute to freeing our government from the grip of Big Money or be faithful to my longtime commitment to help build a truly representative democracy in our nation. Instead, I decided to do what I could to reverse the takeover of the United States by Big Money and corporate America. My goal was to fight their use of wealth and power to buy elections and greatly influence government officials to create and maintain the kinds of conditions that favor them rather than the American people.

When corporate lobbyists for an oil industry making record profits spend millions of dollars to convince Congress to grant their companies unneeded subsidies and tax loopholes, we, the taxpayers, unwittingly foot the bill. Given how well our congressional representatives serve the oil industry, it's obvious why our country has made little progress toward a sustainable, renewable energy policy that would benefit the entire population. And when PhRMA successfully lobbies Congress to enact laws preventing Medicare administrators from negotiating lower drug prices for our burgeoning senior population, it's crystal clear who our elected officials are really working for. Despite such circumstances, American voters continue to elect people to Congress and the White House who look out for the interests of the oil industry, PhRMA, and other large and powerful commercial entities to the detriment of the vast majority of the population.

Breaking Big Money's Grip on America examines how and why this happens, and what we, the American people, can do to build a government that works for all of us, not just those who have big bucks and the most influence. The book makes the case for why a mass movement involving a broad alliance of people and civic organizations from across the political spectrum is urgently needed to save the United States from becoming a plutocracy, a country run by and for the benefit of the very wealthy.

There are a number of reasons for our failure to respond to the increasing threat of an American plutocracy. One of the most critical reasons is our tendency to focus more on how we differ from each other than on how we are similar. Whether due to income, race, religion, ethnicity, politics, sexual preference, age, nationality, or other factors, Americans tend to stay close to those who are most like themselves. This can generate a sense of separateness from others that often creates fear, competitiveness, alienation, and even hopelessness. Instead of coming together to solve our common problems, we fear being taken advantage of and feel we must protect ourselves from Internet scams, burglary, street crime, predator businesses, the government, fellow workers, and even our neighbors. So we remain separate in our own protected enclaves, falsely believing we are safer that way. While we profess to be "one nation under God," we are, in fact, divided in many ways. And the plutocrats do everything they can to keep us divided because they know that if we were to unite we would be much more powerful in our efforts to take back control of our government.

However, some of us realize that on a spiritual or collective level we are all one human race in an interconnected universe. We all breathe the same air and depend on the same planet Earth for our food and water. We have numerous common interests, including supporting ourselves and our families as well as keeping our planet healthy and our communities safe. Focusing on these common interests can unite us in our efforts to keep our country from becoming a plutocracy and serve as a foundation for building political action.

Breaking Big Money's Grip on America calls for this national awakening to our commonality. If we can rise above our feelings of separateness and recognize our commonality, then we could let go of our feelings of powerlessness about our nation's plight. With a renewed sense of purpose, we, the people, could join together in a democracy movement to rid the United States of the encroaching plutocracy that is crushing the American Dream and build the truly representative democracy we have believed in for so long.

Working together to revive our democracy is a monumental task that will require inspiration, coordination, and determination, as well as a myriad of resources. However, I believe it is crucial to take on this challenge and give it our best shot. What will we say to our children and grandchildren if we do little or nothing to save our country from this all-consuming tide of greed and corruption? The ancient Jewish scholar Hillel asked: "If not now, when?" I would add: If not us, who?

PART I

America's Broken Political System

CHAPTER ONE

The Great American Challenge

*Are we willing to stand up to
the power of Big Money and demand
our right to democratic self-governance?*

Today's great American challenge is: can we eliminate Big Money's control over our government before the United States becomes a full-blown plutocracy, a nation ruled by and for the benefit of the very wealthy? If we, the people of this nation, do not aggressively confront this current defining political issue and reverse Big Money's dominance, the American experiment in democracy will soon fail. While some individuals would argue that climate change or income inequality are the great challenges of our time, the chances of our successfully resolving them, or any other major problem, are virtually zero unless we break Big Money's grip on our government.[1] In fact, according to one bipartisan political organization, *74 percent of all voters agree that it is necessary to fix our broken political system before anything can be done to solve other important national issues.*[2]

Big Money's goal is to accumulate wealth and power regardless of the detrimental impact on the nation, the environment, or the people.

Big Money has virtually no conscience and, unimpeded, will continue to exert its powerful influence over government for its own ends with little or no consideration of the consequences. Therefore, breaking Big Money's grip on our government is critical to reviving democracy in this country and improving the lives of most Americans.

America's History Holds the Key to a Solution

While breaking Big Money's grip on our government may appear to be an almost impossible task given how deeply embedded corporate America is in our political system,[3] America's history holds the key to a solution. Time and again when vested interests have constructed seemingly insurmountable barriers to the people's demands for a more equitable society, Americans have come together and overcome the obstacles to a more just and inclusive nation. The most effective method that Americans have consistently employed to create dramatic shifts in society to improve people's lives is mass movements. From abolitionists who fought to end slavery to women suffragists who struggled to establish women's right to vote, from labor activists who attained the eight-hour workday to civil rights marchers who succeeded in outlawing segregation, from Vietnam War protesters who helped end that war to environmentalists who gained many protections for the natural world, people's movements have repeatedly confronted the ruling powers and succeeded in making our country a more equitable place to live for millions of Americans.

Today, the issue is democracy itself. We, the people, are quickly losing our right to self-governance. To prevent this loss from occurring, we need to come together and form the next great mass movement: the Democracy Movement. Such a movement would work to eliminate Big Money's control of our government and place that control in the hands of the people, where it rightly belongs.

Protecting Our Right to Self-Governance

To gain insight into Big Money's daunting opposition to the American people's right to self-governance, it is useful to reflect on a recurring theme in the history of the United States: the people's right to self-determination and desire for a truly representative government. Self-determination is the fundamental right of a people to decide their political status as well as to pursue their own cultural, economic, and social development without interference.[4] Big Money's extensive control of governmental policies has limited the American people's ability to freely pursue these aspects of their lives. In fact, our history has shown that self-determination is not a right we can take for granted. Rather, it is a right that requires continual protection and reaffirmation because it has been constantly under attack by Big Money and corporate America.

Some historical perspective can help us understand the need to protect and reaffirm the right to self-determination in light of our current predicament. On December 16, 1773, before the founding of the United States, the Sons of Liberty dumped 92,000 pounds of tea into Boston Harbor to protest the British East India Company's monopoly on the sale of tea in the American colonies, which the British government had sanctioned. The American colonists' rebellious action became known as the Boston Tea Party. Determined to have a voice in how England governed the colonies, they famously demanded, "No taxation without representation" and refused to pay the duty imposed by the British government.

Less than three years later, on July 4, 1776, the founders of our country declared their freedom from Great Britain. In the Declaration of Independence, they stated that "all men [and women] are created equal, that they are endowed by their Creator with certain unalienable Rights," and "[t]hat to secure these rights, Governments

5

are instituted among Men, deriving their just powers from the consent of the governed...." Our nation's founders asserted that the people are the source of the government's power. No longer would the colonists tolerate a distant king controlling their lives. Consequently, they went to war against the British Empire to gain the right to self-governance.

Almost a century later, in 1863, when the unity of the nation was at stake in the midst of the Civil War, President Abraham Lincoln traveled to the bloody battlefield of Gettysburg and pleaded that Americans "take increased devotion" to the cause of democracy. Lincoln prayed that "these dead shall not have died in vain," that the United States "shall have a new birth of freedom ... and that government of the people, by the people, for the people shall not perish from the earth."[5] More than 600,000 Americans died in the Civil War to preserve the lofty aspirations of our nation and to establish the right to self-governance for African American people as well.

In the twentieth century, our right to self-determination and representative democracy was threatened by Nazi Germany and the Japanese Empire during World War II. Along with many other nations, the United States fought to maintain its freedom from foreign domination. Tens of thousands of Americans lost their lives and many more were injured to protect our democratic way of life.

Now, in the twenty-first century, we have a new challenge to our right to self-governance and representative democracy, one that is perhaps not as obvious but just as great as those of the past. As with the Civil War, the current threat comes from within and is of our own making. Since the American people have not yet organized any significant resistance to Big Money's grip, it has steadily taken increasing control of our government.

Surely the colonists, revolutionists, and other Americans who engaged in subsequent battles did not fight and die so that giant multinational corporations could one day rule our country. Those brave Americans did not sacrifice their lives so that a powerful oil industry could gain a nearly total monopoly on automotive fuel and make $100 billion dollars in profit in 2013 while millions of average Americans struggled to heat their homes and fill their gas tanks.[6] Neither did thousands of America's family farmers fight and die in those wars so that Monsanto and other agrochemical corporate giants could prevent their descendants from saving seeds from their own harvests to sow the following year unless they paid an annual "rental fee" for them.[7] Nor did Americans make the ultimate sacrifice in those wars so that Wall Street banks and other financial institutions could make fortunes creating risky, unregulated mortgage instruments that led to the bursting of the housing bubble and millions of people losing their homes and jobs in the Great Recession of 2008. Something is terribly amiss in our country when we allow such gross injustices to exist and do little or nothing to correct them.

The Curse of Unbound Capitalism

It is the curse of unbound capitalism that America's factory workers, farmers, housewives, machinists, shopkeepers, and others have toiled to build, or fought to preserve, democracy in our country only to have the economic elite reap disproportionate financial benefits while tens of millions of Americans barely get by, many others are homeless, and over 15 percent live in poverty.[8] This curse of unbound capitalism actually goes beyond the tremendous financial disparity between the economic elite and the rest of society. The fact is we live in a country that is largely run by and for the benefit of the very wealthy—a plutocracy. As we will see in the coming chapters, the huge amount of money that this small, privileged group pours into election campaigns and lobbying in Washington, as well as in states all across the country, produces laws and regulations that overwhelmingly favor them. In the last thirty to forty years, Big Money's influence in crafting our country's electoral laws and campaign procedures has significantly restricted the average American citizen's ability to have any real effect on the political process.

Consequently, if we, the people of this nation, want to have a meaningful voice in the policies that affect our lives and the future of our country we must join together and develop a way to break Big Money's grip. Otherwise, the super wealthy and corporate elite will strive to increase their already firm hold on our government, keeping most Americans' lives and fortunes under their thumb.

The American Spirit

When the founders of the United States pronounced their independence from Great Britain, they were declaring their right to be free of control by a mighty foreign power. They firmly believed that they were "endowed by their Creator with certain unalienable Rights, that among these are Life, Liberty, and the pursuit of Happiness."[9] Their faith informed them that a higher authority, one greater than themselves or the British Empire, mandated their right to independence. Today, it is imperative that we declare our right to be free of control by a mighty domestic power—Big Money—and to exercise our unalienable rights to life, liberty, and the pursuit of happiness.

Deep inside we instinctively know what is right and just, not from books or teachers but from that place within us that connects to that which is greater than our individual beings. Some would call it "spirit." Though we may or may not believe in God or a Supreme

Being, most of us sense this spirit, which infuses us with life and is part of a greater energy that keeps the planets spinning around the sun and maintains order in the world. This spirit demands that we be self-respecting, independent beings and leads us to believe that we have the right to self-determination.

The story of Rosa Parks illustrates how spirit can give us courage and move us to do what we know in our hearts is right, despite potential dire consequences. On December 1, 1955, this black seamstress boarded a city bus in Montgomery, Alabama, and sat down near the front. When the bus driver ordered her to give up her seat to a white man and move to the back of the bus as was the custom, Parks refused. Her action, insisting that she had the same right and dignity as a white person, ignited the Montgomery Bus Boycott, a pivotal event that triggered the civil rights movement. Parks's courageous decision to oppose the dominant white Southern society and demand equal treatment helped to fundamentally change America.[10]

We each have the same ability to demand our right to equal treatment as Rosa Parks did. But do we have the courage and commitment to oppose the dominant force in our society making the rules that undermine our self-determination? Luckily, we have something that Rosa Parks did not have when she sat by herself in that Montgomery bus. We have each other. We, the American people, cannot forget that what personally affects some of us impacts all of us. When our neighbor is robbed, our security is at risk as well. When employers do not pay their workers a living wage, our tax dollars go to support low-income earners with government benefits like food stamps. When corporations that greatly benefit from government programs do not pay their fair share in taxes, the government lacks funds for projects like the maintenance of roads and bridges, resulting in our cars incurring greater wear and tear and more of us becoming injured or dying in accidents.

At one time or another, we all have moments in which spirit speaks to us. We may experience such moments while praying, hiking, meditating, or simply breathing in the cool fresh air on a sunny afternoon. It gives us a feeling of being connected to others or our surroundings and, when we are really open, to the entire world and universe. In these critical times, we have the opportunity—actually, the responsibility—to embrace that sense of connectedness as Americans so that we can gain a better perspective on how to once again pursue self-determination and democracy in our nation.

We Are All in This Together

By nature, we are communal beings. We naturally create communities, both locally and nationally, for comfort, security, and a number of other purposes. As a national community, we have a common bond that we affirm when we pledge allegiance to our flag: "One nation under God, indivisible, with liberty and justice for all." Underlying that pledge is our spirit of unity—we are all in this together. It is our sense of connectedness as Americans that has given us the strength and courage to win world wars and overcome other great difficulties.

In the late 1960s, I felt this spirit of connectedness while marching in New York City against the Vietnam War. Hundreds of thousands of Americans had come together: young and old; black, white, Hispanic, and other ethnicities; Republicans and Democrats; executives and laborers; veterans and peaceniks. Even though I knew only the few friends who were protesting alongside me as we marched to the United Nations Plaza, we were all united in our resistance to the war and shared a desire for peace and a love for humanity. I knew in my heart that what I was doing was right and felt a higher authority guiding us.

It is with this same spirit that Americans can come together in the Democracy Movement. We can put aside our differences of political affiliation, class, culture, and race for the sake of reviving our democratic way of life. In fact, if we do not join hands soon and break Big Money's grip on our government we will become a nation of worker bees in service to the economic elite now taking control of our country. Consequently, we face not only a monumental political issue but also a moral and spiritual test. As an American community, can we rise up and break Big Money's grip on our government?

Will we answer the call to revive our democracy for our own protection and self-dignity, as well as for the sake of our children and future generations? This is the great American challenge of our time.

CHAPTER TWO

Big Money at the Helm

*Do our elected officials truly represent
the interests of the American people?*

The American people's right to self-governance is on life support. Of the 320 million plus people who live in the United States, every citizen eighteen years of age or older has the right to vote and participate in our democracy. In theory, our elected officials work for us, the American people. But here's the catch: just because we elect our representatives doesn't mean they represent our needs and desires. In fact, they represent the interests of their Big Money sponsors.[1]

The System Is Rigged

The fact that Congress is controlled by Big Money and corporate lobbyists was made clear during the debate over the passage of the 2015 omnibus budget bill. Senator Elizabeth Warren (D-MA), who led the fight against the Wall Street bailout provision in the bill, explained the situation in a way that reveals how our government actually works.

I come to the floor today to ask a fundamental question—who does Congress work for? Does it work for the millionaires, the billionaires, the giant companies with their armies of lobbyists and lawyers? Or does it work for all of us?

People are frustrated with Congress. Part of the reason, of course, is gridlock. But mostly it's because they see a Congress that works just fine for the big guys but won't lift a finger to help them. If big companies can deploy their armies of lawyers and lobbyists to get the Congress to vote for special deals that will benefit themselves, then we will simply confirm the view of the American people that the system is rigged.

And now the House of Representatives is about…to vote on a budget deal—a deal negotiated behind closed doors that slips in a provision that would let derivatives traders on Wall Street gamble with taxpayer money and get bailed out by the government when their risky bets threaten to blow up our financial system.

These are the same banks that nearly broke this economy in 2008 and destroyed millions of jobs. The same banks that got bailed out by taxpayers and are now raking in record profits. The same banks that are spending a whole lot of time and money trying to influence "Congress to bend the rules in their favor."[2]

While passing the 2015 omnibus budget bill, Congress voted to eliminate a key taxpayer protection provision in the Dodd-Frank Act entitled the "Prohibition against Federal Government Bailout of Swaps Entities." That provision was part of the 2010 Wall Street reform bill passed to prevent some of the too-big-to-fail bank practices that led to the 2008 Great Recession.[3] In the process, our representatives gave Wall Street speculators the go-ahead to gamble once more so they and their wealthy clients might get even richer. But if their dicey deals go bad Congress will probably bail them out again with our money. Can we stand by and do nothing? This is particularly disturbing because Congress's $700 billion Troubled Asset Relief Program (TARP) bailout of Wall Street with tax dollars was only the tip of the iceberg.[4] According to a study of all thirty-five Federal Reserve and Treasury Department programs, the actual bailout with our tax dollars was close to $4.7 trillion.[5]

How could our representatives vote to guarantee risky Wall Street ventures after what those same bankers had done in 2008 to crash America's economy? As a result, millions of Americans lost their homes and even more lost their jobs. What appears to matter more to Congress, however, are the huge campaign donations Wall Street bankers, corporate executives, and K Street lobbyists give to our representatives to have their legislative needs met. In effect, we have a political system where Big Money provides the bulk of the funds for our representatives' election campaigns. In return, our representatives enact laws that favor corporate America and Big Money at our expense—what amounts to legalized bribery.

Big Money makes it easy for Congress. Their lobbyists write the legislative sections they want, and all our representatives have to do is insert those provisions into the bills. For instance, Citigroup, in conjunction with other big Wall Street banks, wrote the section in the 2015 omnibus bill that restored taxpayer-backed funds for reckless Wall Street ventures like credit default swaps. In the House, 162 Republicans and 57 Democrats voted for the provision, and it passed in the Senate despite the fact that 21 Democrats and 19 Republicans voted against it. Even President Obama threw his weight behind the bill.[6]

Senator Warren is correct in saying that the system is rigged. Whether Republicans or Democrats control the government, the interests of Big Money most often prevail. While some people are living pretty well with a good job or a nice retirement, countless others are on a financial treadmill running as fast as they can just to maintain the same standard of living. Still many others are not making a living wage and barely get by.[7] One out of five children lives in poverty in America, the richest country in the world.[8] Yet we are willing to accept a corrupt political system practicing legal bribery that allows a very small segment of the population to live as though they own the country. And, to a large degree, they do. How else can we explain the fact that between 2009 and 2012 the incomes of the top 1 percent of citizens climbed 31.4 percent—or 95 percent of the total gain—while incomes of the other 99 percent grew only 0.4 percent?[9]

Moreover, the 2015 omnibus budget bill also significantly enhanced Big Money's ability to influence the outcome of elections in the future by increasing the amount of money a single wealthy donor can give to national party committees each year from $97,200 to $777,600. House Minority Leader Nancy Pelosi rightly blasted the provision, saying it would "drown out the voices of the American people and massively expand the role of big money in our elections."[10]

While this latest budget battle was another victory for Big Money, it starkly exposed the severity of the problem of Big Money's grip on our government and strengthened the resolve of those who want to break Big Money's grip. Consequently, Congress's unwillingness to stand up to Wall Street and its additional support for big donors' influence in elections may well provide a boost to the budding Democracy Movement.

Furthermore, Big Money's control extends to the presidency and the executive branch of government as well. President Obama's antidemocratic tactics used to "fast-track" the Trans-Pacific Partnership (TPP) trade deal through Congress demonstrate the power Big Money and corporate America have over the White House. Since the president classified the TPP negotiations, members of Congress could read the proposed agreement but were forbidden to convey information about it to their constituents or anyone else. Nevertheless, more than five hundred corporate "trade advisors" were given access to the text of the agreement. Many of the negotiators themselves were past or probably future corporate attorneys or executives, but "stakeholder" groups, such as labor unions, environmental groups, consumer groups, health groups, and food-safety groups, were excluded from the negotiating process. Consequently, the agreement will likely tilt the power balance further in the direction of corporations and billionaires, making it even more evident that the president and Congress do not really represent the American people.[11]

If Government Truly Represented the People

While Americans see the corruption and dysfunction of their government, they have yet to fully comprehend the enormous extent to which Big Money and corporate America control their government. For example, the Cato Institute estimates that corporations receive almost $100 billion in federal subsidies every year. State and local governments provide another $80 billion or more a year in corporate subsidies. For the most part, these subsidies serve to increase corporate profits since they are often awarded to profitable companies that do not need public funding to finance their projects. In addition, the tax code gives corporations special tax breaks that effectively reduce a 35 percent tax rate to a 13 percent tax rate, saving these corporations an additional $200 billion annually. Adding insult to injury, the fast-food industry pays wages so low that taxpayers must put up $243 billion in indirect subsidies to pay for public benefits for their workers.[12]

Americans do not grasp the extent to which government could better serve their needs if it truly represented them rather than Big Money.

If we eliminated corporate subsidies and had publicly financed elections taking money out of politics, it would greatly reduce corruption and break Big Money's grip on government. With money removed from politics, thousands of hours that officials now spend on campaign fundraising would be freed up for our representatives to serve the public interest. In addition, the elimination of corporate subsidies would make available hundreds of billions of dollars for a multitude of efforts that would aid the American people. Following is a partial list of programs and projects that could be better funded with the savings:

- Deficit reduction
- Early childhood programs
- Education and schools
- Job training
- Homeland security
- Law enforcement
- Medicare and Medicaid
- Infrastructure
- Public employment for people laid off due to budget cuts

- Social Security
- Student grants and loans
- Veterans' health and rehab programs

Government: Corporate America's Puppet

In his first inaugural address, on January 20, 1981, President Ronald Reagan proclaimed, "Government is not the solution to our problem; government is the problem." But what was true then, and even truer today, is that special interests, particularly multinational corporations and the super wealthy, control government through massive campaign donations and lobbying efforts, making elected public officials puppets of Big Money and corporate America. *That* is our real problem.

Following are just a few examples of how Big Money has corrupted our political system and the destructive effects this has had on our nation.

Healthcare Industry Enriches Congress

American consumers often pay exorbitant drug prices because giant pharmaceutical companies buy politicians' votes and lobby Congress to enact legislation preventing the government from negotiating lower prices. If some consumers are not directly paying high drug prices, it's because others are paying for them indirectly through insurance premiums and tax-supported government subsidies like the Affordable Care Act (ACA). Meanwhile, executives at Merck, WellPoint, and other companies that make up the pharmaceutical and health insurance industries are doing quite well as their companies continue to greatly influence our politicians, keeping the country deadlocked over how we maintain the health of our people and who pays for it.

In 2003, intense lobbying by the trade group PhRMA and strong-arm tactics by House of Representative leaders produced a Medicare prescription drug bill, the Medicare Modernization Act, that barred the government from negotiating lower drug prices. It also banned the importation of cheaper drugs from Canada and gave drug companies stronger protections against their less expensive, generic competitors.[13]

The healthcare industry again used its muscle to prevent lower drug prices shortly after President Obama took office. Within a few months of Obama's inauguration, his administration brokered an agreement with the pharmaceutical and health insurance industries so that they would not work to defeat Obama's healthcare reform bill in Congress. In exchange for promises by the pharmaceutical companies to provide $80 billion in future price cuts to taxpayers or to expand coverage, President Obama pledged not to use the government's immense purchasing power to negotiate lower drug prices for millions of Americans.[14] As for the insurance companies, they received millions of new customers with the passage of the ACA. Meanwhile, the "public option," which would have provided an economical alternative to private insurance, was dropped from the reform package, while universal healthcare was never even put on the bargaining table. Either would have been a much better deal for most Americans but not for the insurance industry's bottom line.

Whose interests our elected officials were really representing when they passed the 2003 prescription drug bill and eliminated the public option from the ACA becomes very suspect when we examine numerous campaign contributions to members of Congress. For example, former House majority leader Tom Delay (R-TX) received $78,250 in campaign contributions from pharmaceutical companies in 2003; House Ways and Means Chairman Bill Thomas (R-CA) received $322,514; senior member of the Subcommittee on Health Care Senator Charles Grassley (R-IA) received $217,921; Senate Finance Committee Chairman Max Baucus (D-MT) received $145,372; ranking member of the Subcommittee on Health Care Senator Orrin Hatch (R-UT) received $433,324; and Senator Baucus, a main architect of the ACA who treated PhRMA favorably, received $3.9 million between 2003 and 2009. Finally, in the 2012 election campaign President Obama received $1.6 million from PhRMA after he reversed his position against the mandate requiring Americans to buy private healthcare insurance.[15] With PhRMA and huge insurance companies calling the shots in Washington, it's no wonder that the United States is the only industrial country in the Western world that does not provide single-payer, universal healthcare for its people.

Our representatives routinely vote for bills favored by their corporate sponsors in return for large contributions to their reelection campaigns. Meanwhile, we, the taxpayers, are paying their salaries and expense accounts while they are spending approximately 20 percent or more of their time fundraising for themselves and their colleagues' reelections. Former senator Tom Daschle noted that senators in the last two years of their terms spend two-thirds of their time fundraising.[16] Is that what we elect our representatives to do in Washington?

Extractive Energy Industry Fuels Congress

Americans do not have an abundance of clean, inexpensive, renewable energy because the extractive energy industry—oil, gas, and coal—has a stranglehold on Congress. Former Senate Committee on Energy and Natural Resources chairwoman Mary Landrieu (D-LA) raised over $1.5 million in campaign contributions from the extractive energy industry from 1999 to 2014. In her 2014 bid for reelection, she received over $250,000 as of spring of that year. Landrieu supported the Keystone Oil Pipeline, tax breaks for big oil, and oil and gas exploration subsidies while she opposed alternative energy subsidies, the Environmental Protection Agency's regulation of greenhouse gas emissions, limitations on toxic emission for power plants, and increasing tax incentives for oil companies to develop alternative energy programs.[17]

Senator John Cornyn (R-TX), the former ranking member of the Subcommittee on Energy, Natural Resources, and Infrastructure, received over $375,000 in campaign contributions from the extractive energy industry for his 2014 reelection bid. Since 1999, Cornyn has received $2.54 million in contributions from that industry. Cornyn supports the Keystone Oil Pipeline, tax breaks for big oil, and oil and gas exploration subsidies. He opposes alternative energy subsidies and tax credits, hydrogen fuel cells, clean energy achievement criteria, and an increase in tax incentives for oil companies to develop alternative energy programs. He has a zero rating from the League of Conservation Voters.[18] Many more members of Congress could be added to the list of officials who help keep Americans chained to the extractive energy industry.

A 2011 NBC/*Wall Street Journal* poll indicating that 74 percent of Americans believe Congress should end special tax breaks for big oil companies suggests these elected officials weren't representing the public's concerns.[19] Considering the fact that virtually the entire scientific community points to the burning of fossil fuels as a major cause of global warming threatening humanity's survival makes clear just how tightly our representatives are tied to their corporate sponsors.[20] To make matters worse, these same representatives refuse to examine the scientific evidence, ridicule climate change, and lead their constituents to believe the idea of humans causing global warming is a hoax.[21]

Breaking the extractive industry's grip on Congress is critical to the well-being of our planet and generations to come.

Gun Lobby Blocks Public Safety Measures

The gun lobby also controls our representatives. Since the 2000 election cycle, the National Rifle Association (NRA), the firearms industry, and the Gun Owners of America have contributed a combined $81 million to congressional and presidential election campaigns to defeat gun control measures, according to federal disclosures and a Center for Responsive Politics analysis done for the Center for Public Integrity.[22]

Such opposition to gun control by government representatives occurs despite the fact that over 11,000 people were killed by gun violence in the United States in 2011, according to the Bureau of Justice Statistics.[23] Moreover, 92 percent of Americans support universal background checks for all gun purchases, based on a July 2014 Quinnipiac University poll.[24] Since the 1993 Brady Handgun Violence Prevention Act, Congress has not passed a universal background check statute or any other meaningful legislation to deal with the issue of gun violence in our country. For example, in spring 2013, forty-six senators voted to block any expansion of background checks just four months after twenty-six people, including twenty young children, were shot dead at the Sandy Hook Elementary School in Newtown, Connecticut. Among those voting to block stronger background checks was Senator Roy Blunt (R-MO), who had received $2.6 million from the NRA during his election campaign in 2010. Since 2000 some of the other leading Senate recipients of NRA campaign contributions have been Ron Johnson (R-WI), $1.2 million; Rob Portman (R-OH), $1.35 million; Richard Burr (R-NC), $852,000; John Thune (R-SD), $717,000; and Saxby Chambliss (R-GA), $355,000.[25]

Though 92 percent of Americans want universal background checks for people purchasing guns, our elected officials' personal ambitions override the public interest and dictate their political actions.[26] Such statistics make clear the fact that the gun lobby's Big Money controls our Congress.

Defense Contractors Reward
Their Congressional Supporters

The positions of our representatives are also influenced by the defense sector. Between 1989 and 2010, Lockheed Martin, the government's biggest defense contractor, contributed $19.3 million to federal political campaigns.[27] Senator Dick Durbin (D-IL), who until January 2015 chaired the Senate Defense Appropriations Subcommittee, received $74,200 from Lockheed Martin from January 1, 2001, to December 31, 2013, 4.8 times the average for a US senator. During the same time period, Representative Rodney Frelinghuysen (R-NJ), chair of the House Defense Appropriations Subcommittee, accepted $66,500 from Lockheed Martin, 4.4 times the average for a representative. The subcommittees chaired by Senator Durbin and Representative Frelinghuysen in the Senate and House, respectively, are where funding for defense projects originate. In the 2013 to 2014 campaign cycle alone, through June 30, 2014, Senator Durbin received $242,399 in contributions from the defense sector. Over the same period, Representative Frelinghuysen's donations from defense contractors amounted to $208,981.[28]

Meanwhile, Representative Kay Granger (R-TX), who is currently vice chair of the House Appropriations Subcommittee on Defense, received $226,150 from Lockheed Martin during the 2013–2014 campaign cycle through June 30, 2014, more than any other current member of Congress. In November 2011, Representative Granger joined with Representative Norm Dicks (D-WA), the ranking member on the House Appropriations Committee, to form the bipartisan Joint Strike Fighter (JSF) Caucus ostensibly to provide members of Congress with information on the development of the new F-35 fighter jet, the most expensive program in Pentagon history.[29] However, it appears that in reality the JSF Caucus was formed to promote the continued funding of this extremely over-budget project. Not surprisingly, the four primary contractors building the F-35, including Lockheed Martin, contributed a total of $326,400 to members of the caucus in 2011, which, per member, is nearly double what they gave to the average representative not in the caucus. Moreover, caucus members received campaign contributions from employees of these defense contractors that were nearly double the amount that non-caucus representatives received from these same employees. And the two co-chairs of the caucus, Granger and Dicks, received the largest campaign contributions from the contractors. Clearly, the defense contractors were rewarding caucus members for their efforts in support of the fighter jet project. At the same time, their generous contributions were helping to ensure future congressional support for the JSF and other defense projects.[30]

By July 2014, the cost of the JSF project, which in 2001 had been projected to be $233 billion, had ballooned to $398.6 billion. A portion of those funds could have been used to rebuild the country's crumbling roads and bridges, provide funding to lower interest rates for thousands of financially strapped college students, or prevent cuts in the Food Stamp Program for needy families. Though the JSF project created some jobs, many more could have been developed through nondefense economic stimulus packages.[31]

But since college students, food stamp recipients, and the jobless do not have the financial resources and lobbying power that defense contractors possess, their needs do not get anywhere near the attention and funding from Congress that these special interests do. *As Congress lavishes funds on special interests like the JSF while, at the same time, receiving generous campaign contributions from these same interests, basic needs of millions of Americans go unmet.*

The Rise of Corporate Political Power

Corporate efforts to influence government policies and the direction of our country, while rapidly increasing in the United States today, are not a new phenomenon. In *The Web of Debt*, Ellen Hodgson Brown explains that the nineteenth-century Populists, who represented the interests of the common man, "saw their antagonist... as the private money power and the corporations it had spawned, which were threatening to take over the government unless the people intervened."[32]

In fact, the birth of our nation is rooted in the struggle between the people and government-sanctioned corporate power. As noted in chapter 1, when the American colonists dumped massive amounts of tea into the harbor at the Boston Tea Party of 1773 they were resisting not only the British government's tea tax but also that government's support of the East India Company's monopoly on the sale of tea in the colonies.[33]

In *When Corporations Rule the World*, David C. Korten rightly asserts that corporations in the United States have been engaged in a process of restructuring the rules and institutions of governance to suit their interests for more than 150 years.[34] During the age of the Robber Barons in the late 1800s, men like John D. Rockefeller, J. Pierpont Morgan, Andrew Carnegie, James Mellon, and Cornelius Vanderbilt built great wealth by manipulating state and federal governments into adopting laws and rules that favored their corporate interests over the common good in spheres such as tariffs, banking, railroads, labor, and public lands.[35] And in the 1930s, President Franklin D. Roosevelt warned the American people about the influences on government of powerful individuals and groups when he said:

> The first truth is that the liberty of a democracy is not safe if the people tolerate the growth of private power to a point where it becomes stronger than their democratic state itself. That, in its essence, is fascism—ownership of government by an individual, by a group, or by any other controlling private power.[36]

A pivotal moment in the rise of corporate power occurred in the 1886 case of *Santa Clara County v. Southern Pacific R. Co.*, 118 U.S. 394. When the US Supreme Court rendered its decision, the Court reporter inserted a headnote stating that the sense of the Court's decision was that a private corporation has the same rights as a person under the equal protection clause of the Fourteenth Amendment to the US Constitution, even though the Court had not specifically addressed this issue.[37] This line of legal reasoning culminated in the 2010 case of *Citizens United v. Federal Election Commission*, 558 U.S. 310. In this decision, the US Supreme Court held that money is speech and that the freedom of speech clause of the First Amendment prohibits the government from restricting independent political expenditures by corporations, associations, or labor unions. Corporations can now spend as much as they want to influence the outcome of elections as long as they do not contribute directly to candidates. The *Citizens United* ruling greatly diminished the voting power of individuals by granting corporations immense financial influence in determining the outcome of elections. Consequently, the reality is that a handful of Americans, many of whom sit on the boards of corporations, determine corporate expenditures that significantly influence election campaigns. And extensive lobbying by these corporations results in laws and policies favoring corporate interests that are contrary to the public interest.

> *It is fair to conclude that we do not have a government of, by, and for the people. Rather, the United States, for the most part, is a government of, by, and for Big Money and corporate America.*

CHAPTER THREE

America Out of Balance

*In the public policies of a democratic society,
shouldn't the common good receive at least as much
consideration as the interests of big business?*

Almost a century ago, Calvin Coolidge clearly articulated the important role of business in American society. In a speech to the Society of American Newspaper Editors on January 17, 1925, President Coolidge observed, "The chief business of the American people is business."[1] As president, Coolidge promoted his view of America by reducing government regulation of corporations, supporting subsidies for industries, protecting American business with high tariffs on imported products, and cutting taxes. The business community applauded these policies because, among other effects, they fueled a boom in the stock market.

Like today's Republican Party, President Coolidge believed in allowing business the widest possible range in which to operate. In fully supporting private enterprise, he placed his faith in the self-regulation of the marketplace and the "trickle-down" theory of prosperity, the notion that prosperity for corporations and the upper echelons of society positively affects the lower levels of society as well. While many in today's Democratic Party would argue that issues such as education, the environment, health care, and support for the middle class are important regardless of which party occupies the White House, the government almost always gives the interests of business and the economy maximum consideration.

Of course, economic growth is by and large good for a nation. This is particularly true in a capitalist country like the United States, where a thriving economy is required to maintain a high rate of employment. However, another important factor underlying the government's apparent preoccupation with corporate America is Big Money's overwhelming influence on Congress, a situation that has rendered America out of balance. Over the past forty years, policy choices that favored Big Money and the growth of finance, while promoting the decline of unions, have led to the great rise in income inequality that has largely contributed to America's being out of balance. Income inequality in the United States is now at its most elevated since 1928. Starting in the mid- to late-1970s, the uppermost tier's pretax income share began rising rapidly. In 2012, the top 1 percent received nearly 22.5 percent of all pretax income, while the bottom 90 percent's share was below 50 percent of pretax income for the first time ever.[2] Further, 95 percent of all income between 2009 and 2012 went to the top 1 percent of the population.[3]

Although various jobs have greater or lesser value and should be rewarded accordingly, all people who contribute to society with their dependable labor deserve decent pay for their efforts. But the need for balance goes even beyond that. Whether in our personal lives, our communities, our country, or the entire world, balance is essential to success and a positive state of being.[4] In terms of America, this means balancing our focus on business with support for such things as education, health care, the arts, and the environment. In *Humanism: Beliefs and Practices,* Jeaneane Fowler writes that the key to the future lies in "well-balanced relationships in personal, societal, and global existence."[5] Unfortunately, the more unbalanced American society becomes the dimmer our future looks.

In Buddhism, balance is portrayed as the Middle Way, a path of moderation between the extremes of self-indulgence and austerity.[6] In Western religion, balance is the "spiritual straightness and stability that resists all influences to turn or deviate from the right path."[7] While Big Money adheres to the goal of maximizing profits and individual gains, the principle of balance teaches us that society is "more stable when different elements are in the correct or best possible proportion."[8] Surely our lives would be enhanced and America a better place to live if the principle of balance guided our political process and public policies. By breaking Big Money's grip, we can at least balance the public good with the interests of corporate America.

Assessing America's Imbalance

The following examples demonstrate how out of balance America is due to policies that heavily favor Big Money and corporate America.

Healthcare Business Trumps the Public's Interest

There have been many recent examples of how the healthcare industry influenced government policies on health care. In 2009, when the Obama administration proposed to expand the availability of health care and lower its cost to the public, it would have been reasonable to assume the president would consult with providers and consumers about the problems with the current system. However, soon after taking office and before presenting any healthcare proposals to providers, consumers, or Congress, Obama and members of his administration met privately with pharmaceutical and health insurance company executives,[9] who then used their considerable power and influence to set important terms of the healthcare legislation.[10] Rather than rallying the American people to support universal healthcare—much more in the public's interest and the approach adopted by practically all other Western industrialized nations—President Obama bowed to the interests of big business. It was government as usual. Our newly elected president failed to keep his campaign promise of "change we can believe in."

Then to make matters even worse, Senator Max Baucus (D-MT), chairman of the Senate Finance Committee, recruited his former health policy aide, Elizabeth (Liz) Fowler, to draft the Affordable Care Act (ACA). Since working for Senator Baucus, Fowler had become vice president for Public Policy and External Affairs of WellPoint (now Anthem), the nation's largest private insurer. In effect, Senator Baucus hired an industry lobbyist to write the healthcare legislation. It's hard to imagine a clearer conflict of interest.[11] The final version of the bill strongly favored the insurance industry since it required every American to buy private health insurance with no alternative public option provided by the government.

Moreover, after the Affordable Care Act passed, the Obama administration turned to Liz Fowler to oversee its implementation. Thus, not only did a health insurance executive write the ACA but that same health insurance insider ensured that the law was implemented with the industry's interests in mind. No one in the White House seemed to have a problem with the ethical implications of Fowler being put in charge of the people's healthcare law.[12] Nevertheless, this was a blatant example of not only the government working for corporate America at the people's expense but also the revolving door between business and government that further enables Big Money's grip on government.

The Fowler-ACA saga demonstrates the entrenched bias in our governmental system. When Fowler left the White House after a stint as special assistant to the president for health care and economic policy she went back through the revolving door to private industry, taking a senior-level position with Johnson & Johnson's government affairs and policy group.[13] With all her government contacts, Fowler will undoubtedly be able to help Johnson & Johnson get the policy preferences it wants from our government. Unfortunately, the American people don't have someone with Fowler's connections backed by Big Money's influence working to counterbalance her weight in Washington.

Obama's ACA legislative maneuvers were not much different from the ones President George W. Bush and the Republicans in Congress employed when Bush proposed Medicare's new drug benefit in the Medicare Modernization Act of 2003. A huge incentive causing the pharmaceutical manufacturers to support the Part D drug benefit was Bush's agreeing to their demand that the federal government not be permitted to negotiate with the drug companies for cheaper prices.[14] Also, the bill made no provisions for covering its cost of over $500 billion,[15] for which future American taxpayers will have to pay. Not surprisingly, the biggest beneficiaries of the new law were PhRMA and the insurance companies. Once again the government did corporate America's bidding with little regard for the tax-paying public or the elderly.

Energy Industry Prevails over the Common Good

There have also been many recent examples of how the energy industry has influenced government policies in directions not conducive to the common good. For instance, within weeks of his inauguration in 2001, President George W. Bush appointed Vice President Dick Cheney to chair the National Energy Policy Development Group (NEPDG) with the mission of formulating a new energy policy for the country. Having served from 1995 to 2000 as chairman and CEO of Halliburton, one of the world's largest oil services companies, Cheney strongly favored oil and other traditional sources of energy. The vice president proceeded to hold secret talks with energy industry executives while drafting the nation's new energy policy, a plan that benefited the industry much more than it did the long-term interests of the American people.

According to a *Los Angeles Times* article dated August 26, 2001, Cheney's task force consulted extensively with corporate executives while environmental groups had little input:

> Many of the executives at the White House meetings were generous donors to the Republican Party, and some of their key lobbyists were freshly hired from the Bush presidential campaign. They found a receptive task force. Among its ranks were three former energy industry executives and... a Bush agency head who was involved in the sensitive discussions while his wife took in thousands of dollars in fees from three electricity producers....
>
> Cheney and his staff generally heard a message reinforcing their own mind-set: free markets, fewer pollution rules and expanded development of traditional fuels....
>
> The report focuses on easing regulation for oil and gas drilling, coal-fired generators, nuclear power plants and transmission of electricity, while providing energy assistance to poor households. Though the plan also backs alternative

fuels and conservation, it gives the most support to increasing the supply of traditional sources of energy....

Even basic assumptions in the report were tailored to industry's measure....

Environmental leaders say they never got a real chance to influence the report in favor of greater conservation efforts and renewable power.[16]

Evidently, corporate America dictated public policy and the Bush administration made little effort to provide a balanced approach to America's energy policies.

Going to War for Business

Even in matters of war and peace, the government has often put business interests ahead of the public good. A strong argument can be made that the Iraq War was an American war of choice primarily to gain control of Iraq's vast oil and gas reserves. Oil executive-turned-vice president Cheney played a leading role in this underhanded affair as well. Prior to the US invasion of Iraq in March 2003, the Bush administration stated that Iraq was developing weapons of mass destruction (WMD) and that this posed a threat to the security of the Middle East and the West.[17] On February 5, 2003, at the United Nations Security Council, Secretary of State Colin Powell asserted that the United States had solid, factual evidence that a preemptive strike was necessary to prevent Iraq from becoming a nuclear-armed nation.[18] Subsequently, the world learned that the United States did not have proof to support its case and that Cheney and his aides had gone to extraordinary lengths to distort the facts and discredit officials willing to tell the truth. Additionally, attempts by some government officials to present another view and provide balance to the debate over Iraq were suppressed.[19] In fact, "Scooter" Libby, Cheney's chief of staff, was convicted of four counts of perjury and obstruction of justice for his part in the Cheney Iraq travesty.[20]

Significantly, as early as January 1998 the Project for a New American Century (PNAC), which included such future officials of the Bush administration as Donald Rumsfeld, Richard Perle, and Paul Wolfowitz, wrote to then president Clinton calling for the military overthrow of Saddam Hussein's regime in Iraq to establish international control of its vast oil and gas reserves.[21] Once in office Vice President Cheney had his energy task force examine maps of Iraqi oilfields, pipelines, tanker terminals, and related assets in preparation for an Iraqi regime change favorable to the United States and its allies.[22] With the close collaboration of oil executives, Cheney's group recommended that Iraq be opened to international oil companies. ExxonMobil, BP, and Shell were among the oil companies that played the most aggressive roles in lobbying their governments to ensure that the invasion would result in an Iraq open to foreign oil companies.[23]

While the United States did accomplish regime change in Iraq, the international oil companies did not realize the business boom they had envisioned. Political instability and violence in Iraq have continued following US military withdrawal from the country. The prospects of big oil achieving its goal of exploiting Iraq's natural resources were all but gone. Tragically, hundreds of thousands of Iraqi civilians lost their lives, and the war contributed to the deaths of a great many more people, according to the Costs of War Project by the Watson Institute for International Studies at Brown University. At the same time, in doing big oil's bidding the United States spent close to $2 trillion, lost thousands of American lives, and in effect, bred more support for the militants.[24] If the Bush administration had listened to other views on Iraq and taken a more balanced approach, it's quite possible the Iraq War could have been avoided and radical Islam would not be a major threat in the Middle East today.

Wall Street Foxes Guard the Public Hen House

Numerous examples of how the financial sector has strongly influenced government policies and negatively impacted the lives of Americans are also evident. For instance, in the late 1990s campaign contributions from Fannie Mae and Freddie Mac to key congressional members like Representative Barney Frank (D-MA) and Representative Nancy Pelosi (D-CA) appeared to muffle efforts to investigate the loaning institutions' questionable practices. Consequently, the subprime mortgage market was able to expand significantly, providing cheap credit and dramatically increasing the amount of home loans to unqualified borrowers.[25] Subsequently, in 2008 the housing industry came crashing down when a large number of borrowers defaulted on subprime mortgages and the banks could not cover the loans, leading to the government bailout of Goldman Sachs and other investment banks.

In the 2008 presidential campaign, candidate Barack Obama trumpeted "change we can believe in." Once again, however, despite his campaign promises of real change newly elected President Obama failed to demand strong regulations to curb the fraudulent banking practices that had led to the Great Recession. Instead, Obama supported a bailout of banks while providing little relief to the millions of average Americans who had lost their homes in foreclosures.[26] He refused to extract foreclosure relief from the nation's largest banks as a condition for their receipt of hundreds of billions of dollars in public bailout money even though the TARP legislation included instructions to use a portion of the funds to prevent foreclosures.[27] In doing so, the government sided with the interests of big business over the well-being of a great number of its citizens.

We have to wonder why Obama saved the banks while failing to help millions of American homeowners, many of whom had supported his election. Could it have had something to do with the fact that five of Obama's top twenty campaign contributors in 2008 were Wall Street banks, through their political-action committees and employees? Goldman Sachs alone shelled out over one million dollars to Obama's presidential campaign.[28]

Moreover, Obama appointed a number of Goldman Sachs people to important positions in his administration, including Eileen Rominger, the global chief investment officer of Goldman Sachs Asset Management. A large part of Rominger's job at the Securities and Exchange Commission was to protect investors by promoting oversight and regulation of the nation's investment management industry. But the average investor received little protection, and oversight of the investment industry was weak. Other former Goldman Sachs employees Obama named to top administration positions were Larry Summers, Gene Sperling, and Rahm Emanuel.[29] In effect, the president hired a bunch of Wall Street foxes to guard the public hen house.[30]

Some would argue that keeping the big banks afloat prevented the economy from sinking into a depression, which would have made economic conditions even worse for most Americans. While that may well have been true, a more balanced, equitable approach might have been for the government to bail out the millions of distressed homeowners, which the TARP legislation actually required.[31]

Then, with their government subsidies these homeowners would have been able to make their mortgage payments to keep their homes, and the billions of dollars in government funds with which they paid their mortgages would have been deposited in the banks, enabling them to remain solvent. This solution would have helped millions of Americans as well as the banks and mortgage lenders. But once again Big Money's grip on our government prevailed and average citizens lost out.

Big Agriculture Puts Farmers, Consumers, and the Environment at Risk

Agriculture corporations have also greatly influenced government policy, putting farmers, consumers, and the environment at risk. A prime example of this occurred when, on March 26, 2013, President Obama signed into law H.R. 933, the Consolidated and Further Continuing Appropriations Act. A rider to this law effectively barred US federal courts from halting the sale or planting of genetically engineered (GE) crops even if the government failed to approve them and regardless of what the health or environmental consequences might be. Obama endorsed the bill despite a letter signed by over 250,000 Americans urging him to veto it and send the bill back to Congress to eliminate what's been labeled the "Monsanto Protection" rider.[32]

Monsanto Corporation, a major producer of genetically engineered seeds and crops, along with other biotech companies, had effectively lobbied for this provision despite the fact that it puts farmers, consumers, and the environment at risk. In fact, Monsanto had been working for years to find a way around court-mandated environmental impact statements required as a result of a US district court's ruling. The company had averaged more than $7 million per year in federal lobbying expenses over the five years prior to the provision's passage in order to influence decisions in Congress, the US Department of Agriculture, and other federal agencies.[33]

On March 25, 2013, the *New York Daily News* reported that one of the rider's biggest supporters was Senator Roy Blunt (R-MO), who worked with Monsanto to craft the language in the bill.[34] Senator Blunt had received over $70,000 in campaign contributions from Monsanto in the 2012 election cycle prior to the passage of the bill, according to the nonpartisan Center for Responsive Politics.[35] In addition, Democratic senator Barbara Mikulski (MD), then chair of the Senate Appropriations Committee, allowed the appropriations bill with the Monsanto rider to move forward without hearings and without presenting it to the Agriculture or Judiciary committees—hardly a balanced approach. Following the vote, Andrew Kimbrell, executive director of the watchdog group Center for Food Safety, noted, "In this hidden backroom deal, Senator Mikulski turned her back on consumer, environmental, and farmer protection in favor of corporate welfare for biotech companies such as Monsanto."[36] In the final analysis, corporate interests and campaign contributions trumped protecting the safety of farmers, the environment, and the public. Again the government failed to balance corporate benefits and public interests.

If we continue to concede the domination of our government to Big Money and corporate America, then our country will grow increasingly out of balance and our future will become darker. Instead, we need to use the principle of balance to build a better tomorrow for all Americans.

CHAPTER FOUR

The Lobbying Racket

Shouldn't all sides of an issue have an equal
opportunity to be heard prior to our representatives
deciding important public policy?

Lobbying is one of the two most effective tools corporate America and Big Money employ to influence the decisions our elected officials make; the other one, of course, is campaign contributions. The lobbying profession is an extremely large and significant offshoot of big business. According to Wikipedia, there were over 12,000 paid lobbyists in Washington, DC, in 2012. The thirteen top lobbying sectors combined spent almost $29 billion from 1998 to 2010 to influence federal government decisions, excluding campaign contributions, which are arguably just another form of lobbying.[1]

What is perhaps most ironic, even tragic, about the lobbying industry is that American consumers spend huge sums of money through their purchases that corporate America then uses to lobby Congress to pass laws that are in the financial interests of big business and not in the best interests of most Americans. Clearly, the funds that ExxonMobil, Pfizer, or any other corporation devotes to lobbying come either directly or indirectly from the money we consumers pay for gasoline, drugs, or whatever a company's products or services happen to be. That's some racket, and incredibly, it's perfectly legal.

Most Americans don't realize that they're paying for the lobbying racket. Paradoxically, many Americans also donate funds to public interest groups that oppose the legislative initiatives those same special interests promote with the money consumers pay for their products and services, thus inadvertently funding both sides of political debates in Washington.

The financial industry is one of the largest lobbyists in Washington. In 2010, according to an analysis by the Center for Responsive Politics, the industry's lobbying expenses totaled almost half a billion dollars, more than double what it had spent in 2000. During the same period, the oil and gas industry had nearly tripled its lobbying expenditures, spending more than $146 million in 2010. Meanwhile, pharmaceutical companies spent just under $240 million on lobbying in 2010, which was a 139 percent increase over their 2000 lobbying costs.[2]

Lobbying Creates a Huge Imbalance in Governmental Policymaking

Lobbyists can provide a useful service to our government officials, as explained in 1956 by then senator John F. Kennedy:

> Lobbyists are in many cases expert technicians capable of examining complex and difficult subjects in clear, understandable fashion. They engage in personal discussion with members of Congress in which they explain in detail the reasons for the positions they advocate.... Because our congressional

representation is based upon geographical boundaries, the lobbyists who speak for the various economic, commercial and other functional interests of the country serve a useful purpose and have assumed an important role in the legislative process.[3]

However, since lobbyists are nearly always paid handsomely by special interests, be they private industry, the US Chamber of Commerce, or a labor union, the positions they advocate for are clearly skewed in favor of their particular interests. While there are numerous public interest groups that lobby in Washington, their staffs and resources are minuscule compared to those of the huge conglomerates or industry-wide trade associations. According to an April 2015 article in *The Atlantic*, "For every dollar spent on lobbying by labor unions and public-interest groups together, large corporations and their associations now spend $34."[4] Moreover, while some concerned citizens occasionally meet with their congressional representatives to address specific issues, privately paid lobbyists have an overwhelming advantage in influencing our government officials due to the time and resources they have at their disposal. Thus it is reasonable to conclude that the value lobbyists' expertise adds to the governmental process is greatly diminished, perhaps at times even nullified, by the slanted, often deceptive nature of the information they provide.

One example of how the lobbying business corrupts governmental policymaking is the following. In 2009, when the Affordable Care Act was being drafted and debated in Congress, 1,750 corporations and other groups reported lobbying for healthcare reform, according to the Center for Responsive Politics.[5] PhRMA, the drug industry trade group, alone spent over $26 million lobbying Congress that year.[6] A great deal, if not all, of that money came from pharmaceutical companies' incomes from the sale of drugs to consumers. By comparison, the entire annual budget for Common Cause, one of the largest public interest organizations that, among other activities, lobby the government, is approximately $10 million.[7]

In 2009, PhRMA had 185 lobbyists in Washington advocating for its positions regarding the ACA. Seventy-five percent (140) of those lobbyists were former federal employees who had friends and influential contacts in the government; six of them were actually former congressmen. Thus the great majority of PhRMA's lobbyists were part of the revolving door process, which "shuffles former federal employees into jobs as lobbyists, consultants, and strategists just as the door pulls former hired guns into government careers."[8] As a result, the final ACA bill met PhRMA's needs much more than those of American consumers.

The Lobbyists' Revolving Door Invites Bias and Corruption

The revolving door plays a vital role in corporate America's efforts to shape government policy, encouraging policies favorable to corporations and rewarding government officials who foster them. For example, as chairman of the House Energy and Commerce Committee, Representative Billy Tauzin (R-LA) was the primary drafter of the Medicare prescription drug bill, the Medicare Modernization Act, which created Medicare's prescription drug benefit. In his final election for Congress in 2002, he received $174,000 in campaign contributions from health professionals and $119,750 from drug makers and other health products companies. Their investment in Tauzin paid off. The Medicare drug benefit bill he drafted in 2003 "followed the industry's specifications in many respects.... The law steer(ed) clear of price controls and price regulations...and forb(ade) the government to negotiate with drug manufacturers to secure lower prices for Medicare beneficiaries," according to the *New York Times*.[9]

The next year, in 2004, Tauzin left Congress and went through the revolving door to the drug industry. PhRMA rewarded him for writing the prescription drug bill to its liking by making him its president with an annual salary of approximately $2 million.[10] The same year Tauzin left Congress, Representative James Greenwood (R-PA) also retired and followed Tauzin through the revolving door. An influential member of Tauzin's House Energy and Commerce Committee, Greenwood soon became president of the Biotechnology Industry Organization to lobby Congress on its behalf.[11]

When our representatives support legislation that provides huge benefits to corporate America and then leave government to work for those corporations, doesn't it make you question who they really represent?

Several years later, in 2009, as the leader of PhRMA, Tauzin brokered a deal capping at $80 billion the amount drug manufacturers would contribute to President Obama's healthcare overhaul in return for PhRMA's backing of the law.[12] While that agreement helped gain support for the new law, the biggest benefactor was the pharmaceutical industry. Obama traded away the government's right to negotiate lower drug prices in order to obtain the industry's endorsement of the deal.

This drug deal also demonstrates a growing pattern of secrecy in Big Money's interactions with the White House and provides further evidence of corporate America's grip on our government. As we saw with Vice President Cheney's private meetings with energy industry officials and President Obama's classified TPP negotiations, corporate America has the ways and means to get what it wants from the government regardless of what is in the best interests of the American people.

The list of staffers and elected officials who have left their government jobs and then worked for private industry lobbying their former colleagues is long. According to *This Town* by Mark Leibovich, 50 percent of retiring senators and 42 percent of retiring House members have become lobbyists.[13] Among them are former House majority leader Dick Gephardt (D-MO), former senator Evan Bayh (D-IN), and former senator Judd Gregg (R-NH).[14]

After serving for twenty-eight years, Dick Gephardt left Congress in 2005 and formed his own lobbying firm, Gephardt Government Affairs. His clients include Boeing, General Electric, and Goldman Sachs. In October 2012, Rob Epplin, a twenty-three-year veteran Republican Senate staffer, who had been a top aide to both Senator Susan Collins (R-ME) and Senator Gordon Smith (R-OR), joined Gephardt's firm as a vice president. With seasoned former government employees from both sides of the aisle, Gephardt's firm has no difficulty lobbying Democrats and Republicans alike.[15]

Subsequent to serving as the governor of Indiana, Evan Bayh represented his state in the Senate for twelve years. When he retired from the Senate in 2011, Bayh became a partner in the corporate law and lobbying firm McGuireWoods. Among other positions, Bayh became an adviser to the US Chamber of Commerce and Apollo Global Management, as well as a member of the board of Marathon Petroleum. There is little doubt he has maintained his relationships with his former congressional colleagues to the benefit of his private clients.[16]

In 2011, Judd Gregg left the US Senate after eighteen years, plus eight years in the US House prior to that. He went through the revolving door and was rewarded with a position as a senior adviser to the financial giant Goldman Sachs. As the ranking Republican on the Senate Banking, Housing, and Urban Affairs Committee, Gregg had been "a staunch defender of Wall Street and the financial sector throughout the 2008 financial crisis, helping to author the bill that bailed out the nation's largest banks. The finance, insurance, and real estate sector was a top contributor to his campaigns, donating more than $1 million since the 1992 election cycle."[17] Gregg is now the chief executive for the Securities Industry and Financial Markets Association, which lobbies Congress on behalf of Wall Street firms.

While there are some restrictions on lobbying one's former government employer, enough loopholes in the law exist to render the limits practically meaningless.[18] And some former federal officials effectively lobby without actually registering as lobbyists. For instance, former senator Chris Dodd (D-CT) now heads the Motion Picture Association of America[19] and, though he isn't a registered lobbyist, reaches out to his former Washington colleagues on behalf of the motion picture industry. Many other former government officials similarly enjoy extraordinary influence in Washington.

These revolving door examples give the appearance of conflicts of interest and could well be considered unethical. Should former government officials be permitted to use the influence and contacts they've acquired as public employees, paid by the taxpayers, for their private profit? It stands to reason that the public interest should be protected by strict laws limiting or closing the revolving door between government and Big Money.

Doesn't such lobbying compromise the common good, where all sides of an issue should have an equal opportunity to be heard before our representatives decide public policy?

The Revolving Door Is Also Open at the Executive Branch

The revolving door is not limited to the legislative branch of government. In chapter 3, we saw how Liz Fowler used her prior position as a WellPoint vice president to promote the interests of the insurance industry not only in her drafting of the ACA in Congress but also in her implementation of it as a White House aide. Likewise, Vice President Cheney's former position with Halliburton provided a great boon to the extractive energy industry in the development of the Bush administration's new national energy policy.

While in theory it could be argued that the government should utilize people with private business expertise in the public administration of their fields to gain information and perspective, too often businesspeople enter government and end up serving their private industry interests more than the public interest. Robert Rubin is a prime case in point of a successful businessman passing through the revolving door to become a public servant who may have put his former private concerns ahead of the public interest.

In the 1990s, Rubin served as treasury secretary in the Clinton administration after twenty-six years at Goldman Sachs, including more than two years as co-chairman. He and Timothy Geithner, along with Larry Summers, the Harvard economist who succeeded Rubin at the Treasury Department, engineered the deregulation of the financial industry during the Clinton presidency that culminated in the repeal of the 1933 Glass-Steagall Act in 1999. The repeal of Glass-Steagall allowed for the intertwining of investment and commercial banking activities, as had been the practice when the stock market crashed in 1929, prior to the law's enactment. For over sixty years the Glass-Steagall Act had been a successful restraint on overreaching by commercial banks. With its repeal, banks—particularly the big Wall Street banks—were once again able to pour depositors' money into stock market investments.[20] This deregulation set the stage for an unbridled Wall Street boom for big bankers, derivative traders, and hedge fund managers, a good number of whom were colleagues and friends of Rubin and Geithner's. At the same time, their deregulation scheme also laid the foundation for the Great Recession of 2008.[21]

In 2003, Geithner became president of the New York Federal Reserve Bank, where he observed the growing risks in the banking system up close. When Geithner became Treasury secretary in 2009, he oversaw the bailout of the Wall Street banks and contained the financial crisis. However, he failed to break up the big banks and reform the system that had caused the Great Recession. Rather than advocate for the prosecution of those bankers whose fraudulent practices had greatly contributed to the economic collapse, Geithner helped save their skins.[22] As a result, by 2013 his Wall Street friends were doing better than ever while millions of Americans were still struggling.[23]

Geithner was not the only big banker under President Obama. The president appointed a number of Goldman Sachs people to important positions in his administration, which stands to reason given the hefty contributions they had made to his election campaign. The revolving door between the financial industry and the administration ensured that Wall Street's interests were well protected under President Obama.

Unscrupulous Lobbying on the State Level Is Alive and Well
Perhaps the most scandalous lobbying practices take place on the state level. The American Legislative Exchange Council (ALEC) lobbies state legislators around the country to enact statutes favoring its corporate members to the detriment of the public good. According to its website, ALEC is a "nonpartisan membership association for

conservative state lawmakers who share a common belief in limited government, free markets, federalism, and individual liberty." The website explains that "the Exchange Council provides a unique opportunity for state legislators, business leaders and citizen organizations from around the country to develop model policies based on academic research, existing state policy, and proven business practices."[24]

ALEC's lobbying efforts shamelessly corrupt our state legislatures. For example, lobbyists from tobacco companies like Reynolds and pharmaceutical giants like Bayer worked with state legislators to craft tort reform measures that make it more difficult for Americans to sue when injured by dangerous products. In ALEC's education task force, lobbyists from Connections Academy, a large online education corporation, and state legislators drafted model legislation to privatize public education and promote private online schools. It is as if the corporate lobbyists were senior members of the state legislators' staffs.[25]

The Center for Media and Democracy describes ALEC as a "corporate bill mill."[26] Corporations fund practically all of ALEC's budget. According to the Center for Media and Democracy, ALEC has only 1 Democrat out of 104 legislators in leadership positions.[27] While state legislators pay $50 annual dues to belong to ALEC, this accounts for less than 2 percent of ALEC's income. However, each corporate member pays an annual fee of between $7,000 and $25,000 a year. If a corporation joins any of the nine legislative task forces that draft the model bills, it pays an additional $2,500 to $10,000 yearly fee. ALEC receives funding from corporations as well. For instance, it collected $1.4 million in grants from Exxon-Mobil between 1998 and 2009. ALEC has also obtained large grants from some of the biggest foundations funded by conservative corporate CEOs in the country, such as the Koch brothers and

Joseph Coors.[28] Making matters even worse, we taxpayers indirectly support ALEC's efforts to corrupt the legislative process.

Incredibly, ALEC claims it does no lobbying. It has convinced the IRS to grant it tax-exempt status as a 501(c)(3) not-for-profit corporation. Consequently, the Koch brothers as well as ALEC's corporate sponsors can deduct their donations to ALEC from their income taxes just like we do when we donate to the Red Cross or a charity to combat hunger. To gain such status, a corporation must be nonpartisan and do a minimum of legislative advocacy. However, ALEC is clearly a partisan organization and its primary purpose is legislative advocacy.

Corporate influence over legislation via ALEC goes well beyond state legislatures. According to the website Daily Kos, there were ninety-eight known ALEC alumni holding seats in Congress in June 2012.[29] These alumni included House Speaker John Boehner and Congressman Joe Wilson, who called President Obama a "liar" during the State of the Union address. Other ALEC alumni were former House speaker Tom DeLay, Wisconsin Governor Scott Walker, and Arizona Governor Jan Brewer.[30]

As disturbing as the revolving door phenomenon may be to those unfamiliar with how our government really works, tragically it is the norm in Washington today. While we teach our children and proclaim to the world that our country is a shining example of representative democracy, the truth is our government does not represent us.

Isn't it time we demand that our members of Congress and state legislatures represent our interests rather than those of corporate America? Isn't it time we break Big Money's grip on our government?

CHAPTER FIVE

Money Equals Influence and Power

Should Big Money have greater influence in
our elections and over our government's policies
than the voters and the American public?

C ontrary to recent US Supreme Court opinions, money equals influence and power, not speech. In 1976, the Supreme Court found that money in the form of political contributions is speech and, as such, is protected by the First Amendment.[1] Thirty-four years later the Supreme Court ruled in a five-to-four decision that corporations as well as unions are associations of people and therefore also have the right to free speech. Consequently, the Supreme Court held that corporate and union spending on elections is protected speech under the First Amendment.[2]

The highest court in our nation has legitimized the corruption of American politics by Big Money. When the Supreme Court declared that money is speech and corporations are people, we effectively experienced the "doublethink" of George Orwell's classic book, *1984*.[3]

The Court is using misrepresentations and distortions to conceal reality[4]—the reality that money equals influence and power and that Big Money is buying our elections and governmental policies.

The tragedy is that, for the most part, the American people have accepted the Supreme Court's gross distortions of the truth.

To make matters worse, in April 2014 the Supreme Court, again voting five-to-four, expanded the ability of wealthy donors to influence elections by finding that limits controlling the total amount of money a donor may contribute to candidates for federal office, political parties, and political action committees "restrict participation in the democratic process" and are therefore invalid under the First Amendment.[5] The Court's decision in *McCutcheon v. Federal Election Commission* now allows every wealthy American to give over $3.5 million directly to politicians and parties each election cycle, inviting a deluge of funds from a very small segment of the population to greatly influence our elections. In arriving at this decision the Court again made our political process less democratic.

Is Big Money Undermining the Democratic Process?

Somehow the conservative majority of the Supreme Court has come to believe that the spending of large amounts of money by a small segment of the electorate is constitutionally valid, despite the vastly greater access and influence these contributions buy in the political process. In essence, five unelected elite justices have decreed that the democratic process is not unconstitutionally corrupted by extremely disproportionate campaign spending by the super rich. The conservative majority failed, perhaps refused, to recognize that our government, which represents all the people, has a fundamental interest in preventing domination of the political process by the few to the detriment of the many.

In his dissenting opinion in the *McCutcheon* case, Justice Stephen Breyer argued that the Court's decision "fails to recognize the difference between influence resting upon public opinion and influence bought by money alone [and] undermines, perhaps devastates, what remains of campaign finance reform." Breyer further determined that "[t]aken together with *Citizens United v. Federal Election Comm'n*, 558 U.S. 310 (2010), today's decision eviscerates our Nation's campaign finance laws, leaving a remnant incapable of dealing with the grave problems of democratic legitimacy that those laws were intended to resolve."[6]

It is difficult to fathom how the Court's majority did not understand that wealthy contributors like conservative Sheldon Adelson and liberal George Soros gain tremendous access to, and influence over, politicians due to a level of financial support that only a handful of Americans can afford to provide. In 2012, Adelson reportedly gave a total of between $90 and $100 million in political contributions to a number of candidates.[7] And in the winter of 2014 he summoned potential presidential candidates to his home in Las Vegas, Nevada, for private meetings. Clearly, the candidate who eventually obtains his support will feel beholden to Adelson, and, given his wealth, there is no doubt that his opinions will have a much greater influence with candidates and elected officials than those of the average voter.

Another example of extreme influence by the wealthy in the election process are the activities of the Koch brothers, founders of and primary contributors to a conservative Political Action Committee (PAC) called Americans for Prosperity (AFP). AFP's activities were a major factor in the Republican takeover of the House of Representatives in the 2010 midterm elections. The AFP and the Koch brothers also made substantial advertising purchases in a number of 2014 election contests. Many of these political advertisements were focused on defeating vulnerable Senate Democrats as the Republican Party successfully attempted to regain a majority in that chamber. The AFP spent at least $9 million on ads in North Carolina in an effective effort to unseat incumbent Democrat Senator Kay Hagan.[8] Altogether, the Koch brothers pledged to spend more than $125 million to influence the outcome of the 2014 elections.[9] In early 2015, the Koch brothers announced that they intended to raise close to a billion dollars for the 2016 elections from their conservative network of free-market think tanks and foundations.[10]

The super rich on the left also unfairly distorts the political process. For example, in 2013 hedge fund billionaire Tom Steyer spent $11 million to help elect Democrat Terry McAuliffe governor of Virginia. He planned to spend up to $100 million during the 2014 election to support climate change legislation by attacking conservative candidates who oppose such laws, as well as contributing to candidates who favor climate change measures.[11]

Moreover, billionaire George Soros gave $1 million each to two liberal super PACs, Priorities USA Action and American Bridge 21st Century. Soros is now the co-chair of Ready for Hillary's national finance council.[12] Another wealthy, liberal-leaning donor is former New York City mayor Michael Bloomberg, who gave over $8 million to Democratic candidates and liberal PACs in the first several months of 2014.[13]

Nevertheless, the Supreme Court in *McCutcheon* held that the only constitutionally permissible governmental interest served by limiting campaign donations is quid pro quo corruption—that is, the actual or apparent exchange of direct contributions for control of the officeholder's official duties, including an official's votes. Consequently, as long as the government cannot prove that campaign contributions were in exchange for an elected official's decision or vote on any specific policy the government cannot limit these donations.

Big Campaign Contributions Mean Greater Influence

There is, however, new evidence regarding the effect of campaign contributions on elected officials. A 2013 study by the political science faculty at Yale University and the University of California, Berkeley, that included 191 congressional district offices, found that influential policymakers are much more accessible to individuals who have contributed to election campaigns than to constituents in general.[14]

Moreover, the bigger the contributions are the greater the influence. In *The Payoff: Why Wall Street Always Wins*, former Senate staffer Jeff Connaughton chronicles reformers' failed efforts to hold Wall Street executives accountable for the securities fraud and stock manipulation that led to the 2008 Great Recession. His account shows the significant power major donors—in this case, Wall Street bankers—have over Washington politicians and that neither Republicans nor Democrats had enthusiasm for prosecuting the bankers because they wanted to continue raising huge campaign contributions from them, which also explains why Obama's Financial Fraud Enforcement Task Force was merely window dressing.[15]

The book also illustrates how influential senators like former senator Chris Dodd (D-CT) do Wall Street's bidding. In the mid-1990s, Senator Dodd, a benefactor of Wall Street largesse and the ranking Democrat on the Securities Subcommittee of the Senate Banking, Housing, and Urban Affairs Committee, led efforts to pass two major laws that weakened government oversight of the financial markets and softened liability standards for the securities industry. Wall Street and related industries rewarded the senator with more than $900,000 in campaign contributions between January 1993 and December 1997.[16]

One might argue that big contributions balance themselves out so that both parties and their candidates get roughly the same amount of funding. Even if that were true—and it isn't—it would not alleviate the problem of corruption or reduce the overwhelming influence a small group of people has on federal officials. According to the website Open Secrets, "646 people in the 2012 election cycle…hit the maximum overall donation limit of $117,000. This tiny group was able to give a total of about $93.4 million directly to candidates and committees active in federal campaigns." Moreover, "a small number of very big donors (216 people) gave about 68 percent of all the money that super PACs received."[17]

Given politicians' dependency on their donors, it is not surprising that the legislation the majority of Americans desire is seldom what Congress enacts. Politicians know how the system works. To be competitive in today's media-driven elections, they need an extremely large campaign chest. To get sufficient campaign funds, politicians need wealthy donors. If these donors feel a candidate was not, or will not be, responsive to their legislative or policy preferences, then they will likely not provide the financial support a politician needs for election or reelection.

It seems clear that while ostensibly each citizen has an equal vote our elected officials respond more often to their big contributors' wishes than to their constituents' needs and opinions. For instance, in January 2014 a Quinnipiac University Polling Institute survey indicated Americans favored raising the federal minimum wage by a margin of 72 percent, to 27 percent. Even the Republicans polled supported raising the minimum wage, by a margin of 52 percent to 45 percent. Yet Congress has not acted to raise the minimum wage. One reason could be the Koch brothers' funding of a campaign against such action and their desire to do away with the minimum wage altogether.[18] Similarly, in October 2013 another Quinnipiac poll determined that 88 percent of Americans favored a background check before an individual could purchase a gun, yet opposition funding from the Koch brothers, the National Rifle Association, and others has prevented passage of this commonsense measure.[19]

Do We Want a Truly Representative Democracy?

The United States claims to be the greatest democracy in the world. Many Americans pride themselves on our elections being fair and honest. We even send observers to other countries to ensure that their elections are fair and honest by American standards. Yet when a small segment of the electorate can spend huge sums of money to influence voters' opinions about the candidates and big donors, or the super PACs they fund, can run ads that say anything they want about a candidate regardless of whether their claims are true or not, we cannot say our elections are fair and honest.

The truth is our country's elections are not fair and honest.

The crucial questions are: If we want our country to function as a truly representative democracy, can we allow corporations, which by law have the sole purpose of maximizing profits for their shareholders, to have the same rights as people under the First Amendment? And should the amount of money people or corporations contribute to candidates determine the amount of influence they have in an election or with government officials once elected?

Despite the Supreme Court's decisions, a vast majority of Americans would answer no to both questions. In a Legal Progress survey, 56 percent of respondents rejected corporate personhood, while only 25 percent agreed that corporations are people. Further, by a 48-point margin (65 percent to 17 percent) voters believed corporations should not be able to spend unlimited amounts of money in political campaigns.[20]

A Pivotal Moment in American History

We are at a pivotal moment in American history. If the American people accept the Supreme Court's rulings in the *McCutcheon*, *Citizens United*, and *Buckley* cases, then the United States will be a plutocracy. Are we, the American people, going to accept this takeover of our country, or will we have the courage to demand that these decisions be reversed and to take back our government?

The spirit of "one nation under God" is summoning us. But will we recognize our common purpose and face this challenge? As Americans, we all want what's best for our families, our communities, and our country. Now is the time to overcome our feelings of helplessness and separateness, join together to build a powerful mass movement, and defeat our common adversary, Big Money.

We can create a truly representative democracy in America by joining together to build a democracy movement.

PART II

Creating a Truly Representative
Democracy in America

CHAPTER SIX

Building a Democracy Movement

The development of a mass movement is
the one strategy that has most consistently produced
lasting change in the United States.

In part 1 of *Breaking Big Money's Grip on America*, we examined a
number of the most troubling problems with our political system
that are turning our country into a plutocracy. Given this current
state of affairs, can we, the American people, establish in its place
a truly representative, democratic republic in the United States?
Meeting this daunting challenge will require building a democracy movement consisting of millions of Americans from across the
political continuum dedicated to its cause.

Numerous groups, both on the left and on the right, have
been working for many years to significantly alter national policies and redirect the course of our country. None, however, has
developed a message powerful enough to strike a common chord
and engage a broad spectrum of the American public in a mass
movement for fundamental change. Most recently the Tea Party
and Occupy Wall Street have attempted to rally people to their

calls for political renewal, but for various reasons neither has yet been able to inspire the great number of Americans needed for their efforts to succeed.

So what can we do now to create a mass movement for democracy? Before addressing this question, however, it's important to understand why a mass movement provides the best opportunity for successfully reviving democracy in America.

The Transformative Power of Mass Movements

As discussed in part 1, we cannot rely on our elected representatives by themselves to create a fair and just society that works for all of us. Our government officials are too influenced by Big Money to take the bold steps necessary to revive democracy in America. Then again, mass movements have historically proven to have astonishing power to transform society. The bigger the movement, the greater the potential it has to effect change.

However, a movement's power comes not only from its great numbers but also from a common bond among its participants as well as a moral authority underlying its cause. People join a movement primarily because they believe in its cause; they feel a kinship with others in it; and they have a stake in the outcome. A common, greater purpose is a driving force that empowers mass movements. Whether the issue is gay and lesbian rights, right to life, or black lives matter, movement activists feel a deep sense of righteousness about their cause, as if a higher authority has called them and it is their duty to respond.

A Brief History of Mass Movements in America

The defining characteristics of successful mass movements are reflected in their history in America. An early movement in the

United States was the labor movement, which began before the Revolutionary War when journeymen tailors in New York called a strike in 1768 to protest a reduction in their wages.[1] Since then, millions of workers have formed labor unions and organized for what they believed were fair working conditions. Thanks to the demands of the labor movement, American workers have the eight-hour workday, child labor laws, workplace safety regulations, and the minimum wage, among other major workplace advances.

Perhaps the first successful mass movement in the United States was the abolitionist movement to end slavery. Many abolitionists believed in a "higher law" that was greater than the US Constitution, which protected slavery. On January 1, 1863, when President Lincoln signed the Emancipation Proclamation to abolish slavery in the rebellious states, he invoked "the considerate judgment of mankind, and the gracious favor of Almighty God." At the end of the Civil War, the nation ratified the Thirteenth Amendment, ending slavery in the entire country.[2]

In the second half of the nineteenth century and the early twentieth century, the women's suffrage movement struggled to gain women's right to vote. For over seventy years, women organized, lectured, wrote, marched, lobbied, held vigils, conducted hunger strikes, and practiced civil disobedience to achieve the right to vote.[3] Their just cause and the spirit of sisterhood gave women hope that someday they would succeed. In 1920, the movement finally achieved its goal with the ratification of the Nineteenth Amendment to the Constitution, which enfranchised women.

The civil rights movement of the 1950s and 1960s brought millions of black and white Americans together to demand the end of racial segregation and discrimination against blacks, as well as to guarantee their right to vote. Centered in black churches in the

South, the civil rights movement was driven by a strong spiritual and communal energy. It utilized sit-ins and other tactics employed by the women's suffrage and labor movements to obtain its goals, many of which have yet to be fully realized. Perhaps its greatest achievements were the passage of the 1964 Civil Rights Act, outlawing discrimination based on race, color, religion, sex, or national origin, and the 1965 Voting Rights Act, which prohibited racial discrimination in voting.[4]

From the mid-1960s to the early 1970s, the movement against the Vietnam War swept the country.[5] While the previous movements had been focused on gaining rights for, as well as improving the lives of, a particular segment of the population, the anti-Vietnam War movement was focused on changing the government's foreign policy and ending the war. As with other movements, this effort grew out of a sense of moral authority, with most Americans knowing that the killing of thousands of Vietnamese, a great many of them noncombatants, was morally wrong. The Vietnam War, which directly affected the vast majority of the nation, as almost everyone in the country had a friend or relative who was involved in it, became increasingly unpopular as American casualties mounted and there seemed to be no end in sight. After years of protest marches, vigils, lobbying, and civil disobedience, the movement achieved its goal when the United States finally pulled out of Vietnam on March 29, 1973.

The feminist movement, which also began in the 1960s,[6] was initially focused on issues of workplace inequality and gender discrimination. As the idea of women's liberation grew, the movement broadened to encompass multiple aspects of women's lives, from sex to marriage to work. Many women, disillusioned and upset, started consciousness-raising groups in their communities to share their stories about family life, education, work, and sex. They saw themselves in relation to the larger society, discovered their commonalities, and built solidarity. Women wanted justice and equality for themselves and for all women. To borrow a line from the classic movie *Network*, women were "mad as hell, and they weren't going to take it anymore." While women have not yet obtained full equality with men in our society, because of the feminist movement they have achieved major gains in business, education, and culture.

Other important movements include the environmental movement, the related Climate Change Alliance, the gay rights movement, and the peace and justice movement, all of which are still working today for fundamental change. Each has met fierce resistance from the status quo and employed great determination and years of struggle to attain some, if not all, of its goals. Significantly, all these mass movements have common elements critical to their success.

Common Elements Shared
by Diverse Movements for Change

Following are nine elements shared by mass movements for change and the potential corresponding components of the emerging Democracy Movement.

1. **Mass movements have clear missions and goals.** The missions and goals of mass movements have been clear, well articulated, and capable of having a momentous impact. Such missions and goals made it easier to rally people to join these movements. The mission of the emerging Democracy Movement is to remove the corrupting influence of money in politics and make the government work for all citizens of the United States.

Following are six suggested goals for reviving democracy in America.

- To establish mandatory public financing of all congressional and presidential elections
- To enact a constitutional amendment reversing the Supreme Court's *Buckley v. Valeo, Citizens United, and McCutcheon v. FEC* decisions
- To reform and strictly regulate lobbying to level the playing field
- To eliminate gerrymandering of congressional districts
- To enact a constitutional amendment to eliminate the Electoral College
- To establish a national Bill of Voters' Rights

2. **Mass movements are large scale, reflecting strong support.** To be successful, mass movements have needed hundreds of thousands—at times millions—of people, making them visible and robust enough to ensure that their missions would not be ignored.

Widespread support already exists for the mission and goals of the emerging Democracy Movement. According to an October 2012 poll commissioned by the Corporate Reform Coalition, seven out of ten Americans believe a ban on corporate-funded political ads would improve politics in this country. Eighty-four percent of Americans agree that corporate political spending drowns out the voices of average Americans and makes Congress more corrupt. Eighty-three percent believe that corporations and corporate CEOs have too much political power and influence, and that corporate political spending has made federal politics more negative.[7]

3. **Members of mass movements want real change**. People joining mass movements have often been upset, angry, or dissatisfied about how they were treated or the effects the country's laws have had on them or others.

Correspondingly, today Americans across the political spectrum, from members of the Tea Party to Occupy Wall Street, are frustrated with their government and the influence Big Money has on it. Americans have demonstrated that they are disturbed and want real change.

4. **The core issues of mass movements affect people personally.** At the heart of many movements—most notably, the abolitionist, women's suffrage, labor, civil rights, feminist, and gay rights movements—has been the personal feeling some segment of the population had of being treated unfairly. The success of these movements, to a large degree, has been driven by participants being deeply connected to their goals, which inspired them to work harder to attain them. For example, people involved in the labor movement had an emotional investment in improving their work lives. Women in the feminist movement had a heartfelt desire to be treated on an equal basis with men. During the civil rights movement blacks strongly felt they deserved to be treated as equals. Similarly, Vietnam War protesters feared losing their loved ones and neighbors. In each case, movement participants were propelled by deep-seated personal motivations.

Likewise, Big Money's grip on our government personally affects the lives of most Americans by preventing passage or implementation of policies that could improve their living conditions.

5. **Mass movements possess moral authority.** Moral authority helped drive mass movements of the past. For example, people recognized that it was right for women to be enfranchised, workers to have better wages and safe working conditions, blacks to be treated equally, and Americans to stop killing the Vietnamese people, who had not threatened the United States.

Likewise, the emerging Democracy Movement has moral authority since it focuses on establishing a fair and just society in which every American has an equal voice in how our country is governed. When Big Money drowns out our voices, we lose the equality that the Founding Fathers intended in the Declaration of Independence.

6. **Mass movements meet strong resistance from the status quo.** Past mass movements pitted common people against powerful vested interests in the country—business, the military, white society, males, the government, each resisting to maintain the status quo.

The emerging Democracy Movement will doubtless also face strong resistance from Big Money and corporate America. For instance, the oil industry will not give up its subsidies, nor will the gun lobby permit universal background checks, without a vigorous fight.

7. **Mass movements require hard work and financial resources.** Mass movements only achieve their goals as a result of the hard work and perseverance of organizers and followers as well as sufficient financial resources. While efforts of past mass movements required financial contributions, the driving force behind the accomplishment of their goals was the participants' strong commitment to their causes.

Similarly today, a number of nonpartisan organizations are soliciting funds for goals addressing issues that could be part of the emerging Democracy Movement. For example, Move to Amend, founded in 2009, is calling for an amendment to the US Constitution to overturn the Supreme Court's *Citizens United* decision, eliminate the doctrine of corporate personhood, and declare that money is not a form of protected speech under the First Amendment.[8] Represent.Us is working to end the culture of legalized corruption in politics by overhauling campaign finance rules, enacting strict lobbying and conflict-of-interest laws, and eliminating secret political donations.[9] In 2014, the Mayday PAC began organizing to elect a Congress committed to fundamental reform in the way elections are funded.[10] And most recently, Take Back Our Republic (TBOR) was formed to return political power to individuals and end the escalating campaign contributions by corporations, labor unions, and special interests, all of which fuel government spending. With a conservative perspective, TBOR contends "politicians should be responsible to the people and not to self-serving moneyed interests who seek government subsidies and special treatment at a significant cost to taxpayers."[11]

8. **Mass movements bring people together in a context of deeper meaning.** In past mass movements, while many participants had a personal stake in the outcome, they formed communities that took on greater meaning than their individual interests. On some level, people understood that a nobler truth was powering their movement. There was an indefinable spiritual factor at play, a feeling that they were working for something greater than themselves as I felt while marching on Washington during the Vietnam War. I could see that spirit in people's smiles, hear it in their songs, and feel it in my heart.

9. **Mass movements are transformative.** Past mass movements not only succeeded in changing laws to meet their demands but also greatly altered American culture as a result of the new perspective they introduced. In each instance, the movement's participants, as well as their ideas, gained greater respect and stature.

The emerging Democracy Movement would be equally as transformative. If politicians were to pay attention to the voices of the people and make policy based on the people's needs rather than on the desires of wealthy donors, it would create a sea change in our nation's politics and laws.

Obstacles to Building an Effective Democracy Movement

Though building an effective movement to break Big Money's grip on our government is entirely possible, significant impediments must be overcome. Here are five primary obstacles to successfully building the Democracy Movement.

1. **Having many good causes makes it difficult for people to focus on one overriding issue.** People will often come to the Democracy Movement committed to their own particular issue such as immigration reform, law enforcement, or veterans' assistance. Already believing their cause is most important, they will protect it from being marginalized or abandoned. Many advocates will therefore not transfer time or energy from their issue to the more general cause of reviving democracy without being convinced that it will benefit both them and their primary concern.

2. **People focus their attention on individual and local issues.** Most people direct their efforts to issues that affect their personal circumstances, ones that are manageable and where they

feel they can make a concrete difference. While many are aware of bigger issues in the country and the world, people often believe they lack the time or energy to get involved in those matters. To gain widespread support and be an effective instrument for change, the Democracy Movement must be able to assure people that what they are working to achieve is worth the effort and that their endeavors will make a difference in their lives.

3. **The mission and goals of the Democracy Movement are not easily accomplished.** People will join and work for the Democracy Movement only if they grasp the critical value of the movement's mission and goals and see them as achievable. To be successful, the Democracy Movement must outline distinct objectives and present clear and viable strategies for achieving them.

4. **The Democracy Movement may seem irrelevant to people's everyday lives.** People generally get involved in a movement when they feel personally affected by a problem and have a personal stake in its solution. At first glance, people may not readily see how the Democracy Movement will positively impact their daily lives as citizens.

5. **Fear may keep people from engaging in the Democracy Movement.** People might resist becoming involved in the Democracy Movement because they are afraid of losing possessions, relationships, or even their freedom. People are often unwilling to risk what they have for the possibility of gaining something better.

Given these potential obstacles to success, how can we pull together the huge numbers required to create the Democracy Movement?

The way to begin is by recognizing that when money corrupts our political system, it impacts all issues across the board, affecting every citizen. Whether one's primary concern is immigration, homeland security, or too-big-to-fail banks, Big Money utilizes its formidable power and influence to get the results it desires from our government that are most often contrary to the public good.

> *We all must come together for the common good under one over-arching theme: Big Money has corrupted our political system, destroyed our rights as citizens, and undermined democracy in America. Therefore, we must get money out of politics.*

CHAPTER SEVEN

Overcoming Obstacles to Building an Effective Democracy Movement

*The crisis of plutocracy requires
that the American people put aside their differences
and unite to revive democracy.*

In chapter 6, we identified five major obstacles to building an effective democracy movement in America. Here are ways to overcome each of these obstacles.

Obstacle #1: Having many good causes makes it difficult for people to focus on one overriding issue.

Resolution: Joining forces will benefit everyone's cause.
Though a variety of different issues may produce factions in the Democracy Movement, leaders of the movement can demonstrate how uniting under one banner is likely to benefit everyone. The Democracy Movement must embrace many factions in a powerful coalition. Focusing on a particular issue of any participating member or faction might cause friction within the movement and loss of

support from a segment of the general population. Therefore, people should not be pressured to set aside their issues when joining the greater Democracy Movement but rather the factions should be seen as adding strength and breadth to the movement.

To maintain the largest possible coalition, the movement itself must stay focused on the common goals of political equity and breaking Big Money's grip on our government. It should also stress how Big Money is using its considerable power and influence to defeat almost any cause championed by a faction—such as making our communities safer, advocating for better veterans' health care, or seeking more funding for infrastructure repair—because it is not in Big Money's self-interest. For the most part, Big Money focuses on lowering taxes (which means less funding for public projects, including conservative ones like more policing or greater homeland security) and reducing regulation (which often translates into greater potential for public harm). By bringing together millions of Americans promoting various interests, the Democracy Movement will have the capability to counter Big Money's push to derail almost all issues. Then as Big Money's grip is weakened or eliminated, practically every other issue will receive greater attention from our public officials.

Obstacle #2: People focus their attention on individual and local issues.

Resolution: As people begin to understand the crisis of plutocracy, they will more clearly see how this national issue, like their local issues, affects them personally and they will embrace the Democracy Movement.
Although many people are aware of the important issues in the country and the world, their attention is most often drawn toward those matters associated with the immediacy of their individual

lives. As a result, they may be concerned about but not actively involved in large-scale political or social causes. To draw sufficient attention to the rapid disappearance of democracy in America, the Democracy Movement must emphasize that we are in a crisis that requires an urgent response to stop Big Money's grip from tightening any further. Because people are more willing to sacrifice time and energy during an emergency, such as the country's rapid mobilization following the Japanese attack on Pearl Harbor, Americans need to be educated about the grave danger of plutocracy we currently face as a nation.

While Big Money may not yet totally control government policy, in recent years we have seen drastic examples of how much power it exerts. In previous chapters we noted how the oil industry's grip on our government drove the nation to initiate the Iraq War, costing the country trillions of dollars plus the lives of hundreds of thousands of Iraqis and over four thousand American soldiers. We also saw how the financial industry's extreme influence over our government resulted in the Great Recession of 2008, requiring a huge government bailout with our tax dollars. The crisis of plutocracy calls for an immediate, extraordinary response from the American people before we suffer yet another catastrophe.

Obstacle #3: The mission and goals of the Democracy Movement are not easily accomplished.

Resolution: A positive vision of a democracy that works for everyone will inspire people to action.

It's true that the goals of the Democracy Movement are not easily accomplished and most people do not readily become involved in a thorny issue that appears difficult to resolve. Thus the Democracy Movement must convince Americans that by putting aside their differences and working together for the common good they can solve the problem of Big Money's grip on their government. The movement must offer Americans a positive vision of the future that will benefit everyone. People will join and work for the Democracy Movement if they grasp the value of its goals and see them as achievable. Moreover, reminding people of the daunting obstacles prior grassroots movements overcame to achieve their goals will help inspire in them the desire to join the Democracy Movement.

Obstacle #4: The Democracy Movement may seem irrelevant to people's everyday lives.

Resolution: When people grasp, on a personal level, the value of a restored democracy, they will be motivated to act.

Although the Democracy Movement may seem irrelevant to people's everyday lives, illustrating how Big Money's grip on government adversely affects average Americans can persuade them to get involved. People need to feel personally linked to the movement's purpose as well as grasp the value of its potential benefits for themselves and others. The more deeply connected people are to a movement's values and goals, the more likely they are to become actively involved. Like the climate change movement, a democracy movement would need to address issues that both affect most people individually and strongly impact our society as a whole. Thus to attract people and be effective, the Democracy Movement will need to demonstrate how its objectives can improve the daily lives of citizens through the passage of concrete laws and policies that, once implemented, could break Big Money's grip on government.

For example, one way Americans would benefit from the Democracy Movement's success would be the elimination of the constant requests from politicians to donate to their campaigns. If political campaigns were publicly funded, the flood of emails, phone calls, and letters requesting financial support would cease. No longer would people have to throw campaign circulars in the trash or delete a daily barrage of emails. Moreover, freed from fundraising appeals contributors would have more money for other expenses.

More importantly, if the Democracy Movement succeeds the people sent to Congress could represent us rather than Big Money. We would have a government that was responsive to our needs. Many ideas that a majority of the public now supports could be enacted into law if Big Money were no longer able to buy the votes of our representatives. Without Big PhRMA's grip on our government, Congress could remove the ban on the government's negotiating lower prescription drug prices so that millions of Americans could afford their medicines. Likewise, without the gun lobby's hold on our representatives, we could have universal background checks and other measures providing all Americans greater safety from random gun violence. At last, we would have a government that was working for us rather than for Big Money.

Since members of Congress would not be spending a significant portion of their time fundraising, our representatives would be able to meet with citizen groups more frequently to hear their concerns and work collaboratively to address them. Whatever issues people might be confronting—whether immigration, public safety, health care, or another national concern—they would be competing on a much more level playing field with corporate America regarding public policy decisions. And if money were no longer considered speech, Congress would be much better positioned to control spending on campaign ads, including the truthfulness of those ads.

Similarly, if the Democracy Movement were able to eliminate gerrymandering, people's votes for congressional candidates would carry more weight. Congressional districts would be more evenly balanced in terms of constituents' party preferences. People's votes would be more significant because they would more likely be in a competitive district where each vote mattered in determining the outcome of an election.

By the same token, the elimination of the Electoral College would give every vote the same weight in our election for president regardless of where people lived. The concept of swing states would disappear, and all voters would be on an equal footing during a presidential campaign.

In addition, if the Democracy Movement could overturn voter suppression laws, our representatives would be elected by a greater number of voters. In turn, our Congress would be more representative of the greater population, including minorities and other disadvantaged groups, and would most likely address the needs of more Americans.

Finally, we would have a sense of pride in knowing that our country is truly democratic and that we helped rid the government of the corruption that was destroying the fabric of our nation. We would actually be participating in a meaningful political process where our voices were heard and produced results. Thus, we could take great satisfaction in the fact that control of our government was at last where it should be—in the hands of the people.

Obstacle #5: Fear may keep people from engaging in the Democracy Movement.

Resolution: As people join together with others working toward the same goals, they will discover their courage and move beyond their fear. Perhaps the greatest obstacle to engaging people in the Democracy Movement is fear. People hesitate to become involved because they fear being in the public eye, the possibility of punishment, the loss of their freedom, or even injury or death. Such consequences have occurred in previous mass movements. During the labor, civil rights, and anti-Vietnam War movements, people were beaten and put in jail for protesting corporate or government policies. In more than a few cases, activists have been killed for standing up for what they believed was right. From 2011 to 2013, state and local governments arrested nearly 8,000 protesters in 122 cities across the nation for activities associated with the Occupy Wall Street movement protesting economic inequality, corporate greed, and government corruption. Among them were clergy, students, people who had lost their jobs, and former homeowners whose homes had been foreclosed.[1]

What enabled people to subdue their fears, join these movements, and put themselves in harm's way? Clearly, overcoming fear requires courage. For the Democracy Movement to succeed, it will need to emphasize the moral authority, unity of purpose, and spirit underlying the movement that can generate courage in its supporters. Another factor that helps build courage is the support of a great number of fellow participants in a movement. Moreover, people also may need to go inward and seek direction from a higher power. Some leaders and participants in prior movements have relied on spiritual guidance as well as their sense of justice to sustain their efforts over the course of time.[2]

A New National Mission

We have an opportunity to embark on a new national mission at this turning point in American history by actively supporting the Democracy Movement's efforts to revive democracy in this country. A clarion call for the revival of democracy in America, where everyone is politically equal, would instill in Americans a new spirit of hope. It would also give people a renewed sense of pride in their nation, as occurred when America's mission was to put a man on the moon by the end of the 1960s or when President Kennedy envisioned a New Frontier, or when President Reagan announced, "It's morning again in America."[3] The Democracy Movement could be our new national mission that gives birth to an inspirational time in America.

Once awakened to this possibility, are we, the American people, going to allow Big Money and corporate America to control our government and our national way of life? Or are we going to build a powerful, vibrant movement to wrest control of the country from the 1 percent and put it in the hands of a truly democratic government that serves all the people? It is one thing for people to say that they support ending corruption in government, eliminating money in politics and rescuing our democracy. However, it is quite another to become personally involved in making the Democracy Movement a real force for political equality in America. The following chapters examine specifically what the Democracy Movement's clear and compelling message might be; how it can touch people on a deeply personal level; and how it can attract and mobilize the great number of Americans needed for it to succeed.

> *The big question is this: What would it take for you to begin vigorously working to save our country from the jaws of the corporate plutocracy?*

CHAPTER EIGHT

Reviving Democracy in America

*Strong, bold actions are required
to fix our broken political system.*

There are several signs that a nationwide democracy movement is already emerging. One indication is the launching in 2013 of the Democracy Initiative (DI) by five national organizations for the purpose of "building a movement of 50 million to restore our democracy." The founding organizations are Common Cause, the Communications Workers of America, Greenpeace, the NAACP, and the Sierra Club. As of April 2015, the DI had over fifty endorsers including Asian Americans Advancing Justice, the National Education Association, the National Council of La Raza, and the United States Student Association.

The DI's mission is to establish "a vibrant democracy, free of the corrupting influence of corporate money, where everyone can participate fully and freely in our democratic process, where every voter has a voice, and where our policymakers are accountable to the people and the public interest." According to its website, DI "seeks to restore the core principle of political equality. Labor, civil rights, voting rights, environmental, good government, and other like-minded organizations with broad memberships commit to build a movement to halt the corrupting influence of corporate money in politics, prevent the systemic manipulation and suppression of voters, and address other obstacles to significant reform, including the abuse of US Senate rules that allow a small minority to obstruct deliberation and block action on legislation drafted to address the critical challenges facing our nation."[1]

Another indication that the Democracy Movement has already begun is that in April 2015 the National People's Action, Alliance for a Just Society, USAction, and the Campaign for America's Future brought eight-hundred activists together in Washington, DC, and formed the Populist 2015 Alliance.[2] Part of its extensive platform states:

> *We need to close the revolving door between Wall Street and Washington, and expose the entrenched interests that buy our legislators. We need public financing of elections that bans corporate and big money. We must guarantee the right to vote, with easy access to registration and the polls.*[3]

Additionally, the Liberty Tree Foundation was established in 2004 to build a democracy movement in the United States. Its mission is to bring "grassroots campaigns for democratic reform... together to form a united movement for democracy."[4]

Yet another organization working to revive democracy in America is reclaimdemocracy.org. Its vision is "to create a society in which an informed and active citizenry is sovereign and makes policy decisions based on the will of the majority."[5]

Finally, the National Election Integrity Coalition is promoting the revival of democracy in America as well. Its mission is to help foment and evolve a grassroots populist movement to rebuild American democracy and restore justice and government by the people.[6]

Underlying all these efforts is the fundamental principle of citizen equality. The leading figure in the fight for citizen equality today is Harvard law professor and founder of Mayday PAC, Lawrence Lessig, according to whom everyday Americans do not have "the dignity of equal status as a citizen."

When the amount of money a citizen contributes to an election campaign determines the amount of influence that citizen has in our political system, we do not have citizen equality.

Consequently, "the average voter's views do not matter."[7] Lessig could well become the primary spokesperson for the emerging Democracy Movement.

Laying a Foundation for the Democracy Movement

Although the emergence of these organizations is a very hopeful sign, some modifications will be required to ensure the budding Democracy Movement's effectiveness and success. While the Democracy Initiative is focused on creating a network of organizations that share its vision of a truly people-centered democracy, the Democracy Movement must reach out to every American since the more involvement there is in the movement the more power and influence it will have. There are millions of people in our country not affiliated with any organization who would be inclined to support the Democracy Movement if convinced of its importance to them personally. And as the movement gathers momentum, many individuals sensing its moral authority will be drawn to participate. Moreover, to succeed the Democracy Movement has to be more inclusive than the DI or the Populists' 2015 Alliance appears to be. It must be nonpartisan and include a broad range of the political spectrum—Republicans and conservatives, Democrats and liberals, Independents and Libertarians.

Here are some elements that might be included in an effective campaign for building the Democracy Movement. First, the Democracy Movement might draft a "Call to Revive Democracy in America" to be posted on Facebook, circulated by other social media on the Internet, and sent to as many groups and local organizers as possible around the country. This call would need to have a clear and compelling message such as the following:

> *Big Money and corporate America control our government. They buy politicians with huge campaign contributions and persuade them with massive lobbying efforts. We, the American people, are the big losers in this legally corrupt system. We support these same politicians by volunteering in their campaigns, making donations, voting for them, and paying their salaries with our hard-earned tax dollars in the belief that they will support and vote for what is in the best interests of the American people. Yet they repeatedly pass legislation that favors Big Money and corporate America at our expense and to the detriment of the common good. The truth is our government does the bidding of Big Money while it often disregards the public well-being, and Americans are robbed blind by the collusion between Washington and corporate America.*

Second, accompanying the call would be an invitation to join in the Democracy Movement, such as the following:

We invite all Americans, regardless of race, ethnicity, religion, income level, education, gender, party affiliation, or sexual orientation, to join in the nationwide Democracy Movement to break Big Money's grip on our government. We urge all Americans, whether their primary issue is civil rights, the deficit, climate change, the economy, energy, government spending, gun violence, health care, homeland security, immigration, jobs, law enforcement, Medicare, the military, poverty, Social Security, tax reform, veterans' benefits, women's rights, or some other significant cause, to unite in this effort.

Third, a Democracy Movement mission statement and goals to supplement the invitation might include the following points:

The mission of the Democracy Movement is to remove the corrupting influence of money in politics and make the government work for all the people of the United States. To accomplish this mission, we are working to achieve the following goals:

1. Establish mandatory public financing of all congressional and presidential elections

2. Enact a constitutional amendment to reverse the Supreme Court's **Buckley v. Valeo, Citizens United,** *and* **Mc-Cutcheon v. FEC** *decisions finding that money is speech, corporations are people, and restrictions on campaign contributions violate the freedom of speech*

3. *Reform and strictly regulate lobbying so that all Americans have equal access to their elected officials regardless of their income, corporate position, or labor affiliation*

4. *Eliminate the gerrymandering of congressional districts so that each state's delegation to the House of Representatives is proportionate to the votes each party receives in that state's elections for Congress*

5. *Enact a constitutional amendment to eliminate the Electoral College so that every citizen's vote for president carries the same weight and the president is elected solely on the basis of the national popular vote*

6. *Establish a national Bill of Voters' Rights guaranteeing all citizens of the United States an equal opportunity to vote and eliminating restrictive voter ID requirements and other efforts obstructing people's right to vote*

These are fundamental changes to our political structure that will be very difficult to establish. But strong, bold actions are required to fix our broken system and put control of our government in the hands of the people. Half measures will not accomplish what is required.

The "Call to Revive Democracy in America" would be signed by numerous people to give it more influence and weight. Leaders of organizations representing a broad range of issues and political perspectives, as well as prominent people from various professions and trades, would most likely endorse it. Moreover, having citizens from all fifty states sign the call would give it additional force.

Endorsements from organizations working to break Big Money's grip on government and rebuild our democracy would help increase momentum for the Democracy Movement. Therefore, Mayday PAC,

MoveToAmend.org, Public Citizen, Rootstrikers, the National Election Integrity Coalition, Take Back Our Republic, and other similar groups would be encouraged to sign the call and assist in assembling the widest and most diverse coalition of organizations and individuals possible to build a massive Democracy Movement. All these organizations are working hard to eliminate the corrupting influence of Big Money in our political system. (See appendix for their websites and those of similar organizations to learn more about their activities.)

> *The movement's purpose would be to unite everyone seeking to revive American democracy into one coordinated mass movement.*

The Democracy Movement would encourage other organizations addressing issues from law enforcement to education to tax reform to sign the call to join the movement and assist in developing it. Joining together with other major efforts, like veterans' rights and immigration reform, would undoubtedly create a powerful force for change. Everyone who is concerned about Big Money's grip on our government would be urged to actively engage in this work since a coordinated effort to break Big Money's influence would have the best chance of success.

Of course, the Democracy Movement would require financial resources to implement its strategy, including funds for everything from leaflets and phone banks to travel and conferences. Initially the national organization would be responsible for fundraising, but local democracy organizing committees would also be encouraged to raise money to support their activities as the movement would not want to appear to be serving the interests of a few big donors, the very issue it was organized to oppose. The more grass-roots the Democracy Movement is, the more effective it will be.

Creating a Nonpartisan, Grassroots Movement

Because both parties in Congress are closely tied to Big Money, the Democracy Movement would lose credibility and have too narrow a focus if it seemed to be an offshoot of one of the political parties. Therefore, it must be nonpartisan and appeal to a broad cross-section of the American public. Current politicians' campaigns and polls indicate that a great majority of Americans across the political spectrum support reducing, if not eliminating, the influence of money in politics. For example, in the 2014 primary elections, Tea Party-supported insurgent David Brat defeated House Majority Whip Eric Cantor (R-VA) by advocating for, among other issues, getting big money out of politics.[8]

Further, in a July 2014 poll voters by a 65 percent to 30 percent majority believed that the current campaign funding system is wrong and leads to our elected officials representing the will of wealthy donors who finance super PACs. These voters supported a constitutional amendment (73 percent to 23 percent) to overturn the *Citizens United* ruling that money is speech and corporations are people. Independent voters favored such an amendment by a 56-point margin, and Republicans favored it by a 26-point margin.[9] In addition, a Fund for the Republic poll found that 90 percent of American voters think it's important to reduce the effects of money in politics.[10]

Consequently, to tap into the broad spectrum of support for its mission the Democracy Movement needs to work at the grassroots level. Local organizing not only helps build the spirit of a movement but also serves in developing broad-based backing for political equity across party lines, which will be essential for reducing the influence of money in politics and enacting strong campaign finance measures.[11]

Eliminating Gerrymandering

For the Democracy Movement to achieve its mission of removing the corrupting influence of money in politics and making government work for everyone, it cannot focus only on Washington since state governments also foster inequities. With this in mind, gerrymandering, the practice of manipulating the boundaries of electoral districts to favor one party, must be eliminated.

The unfair advantage gained by gerrymandering can be illustrated by the following examples. Under Article 1, Section 2 of the Constitution, Congress has the power to apportion representatives "among the several States... according to their respective numbers." After the national census every ten years, each state is allotted a certain number of congressional districts based on its population relative to the national population. Each state then determines where the lines are drawn between districts within its borders to create that state's appropriated number of districts. In the 2010 elections, the Republican Party made major gains in state legislatures and governorships across the country. Consequently, in a number of state governments controlled by the Republican Party, Republicans practiced gerrymandering by redrawing their states' congressional district boundaries to give their party disproportionate representation in the US House of Representatives.[12] This gerrymandering gave Republicans an unfair advantage in the 2012 elections.

Consequently, the Democrats lost the 2012 elections for the House of Representatives despite the fact that they received 1.4 million more votes than Republicans across the country. Republicans won 234 House seats to 201 seats for the Democrats because of the gerrymandering of district boundaries by Republican-controlled state governments following the 2010 census. More specifically, while the Democrats won the overall House of Representatives vote in North Carolina by 51 percent to 49 percent, Democrats captured only four seats and Republicans took nine seats. Likewise, while Ohio Republicans garnered just a slight majority, 52 percent of the vote, in House of Representatives races, they nevertheless won twelve of the sixteen House seats. Similarly, disproportionately large Republican delegations were elected in Michigan, Pennsylvania, and Wisconsin in 2012 despite strong Democratic turnout in those states. If districts had been drawn according to a nonpartisan process, these tremendous discrepancies would not have occurred.[13]

Gerrymandering is used by Democrats as well. As Ralph Nader recently noted, "The curse of the Democratic Party is gerrymandering that keeps them in office without adequate challenge, never mind from the Republicans, but their own gerrymandered district... They're very, very satisfied, very complacent, very sure that they can continue going to work every day, but they don't have that sense of perceived injustice and empathy that would rouse the public. They're not rousing the public. They're pursuing their own careers and grumbling about the Republicans..."[14]

The Democracy Movement must work to have the people of each state fairly represented in its congressional delegation. When congressional district maps are redrawn after the 2020 elections, they must ensure that each party is represented in proportion to its relative voting strength in each state, as indicated by the 2020 election results. We cannot allow Republicans or Democrats to manipulate redistricting so that we, the people, are not fairly represented. Therefore, if 45 percent of the people in a state vote for a particular party's candidates to represent them in Congress, districts should be drawn so that party has approximately 45 percent of the state's delegation in the House of Representatives.

Perhaps the best way to achieve equitable distribution of a state's congressional representatives would be to have the district boundaries drawn by a redistricting commission instead of state legislatures, which are almost always controlled by one or the other party. In the 2014 election, New York became the fourteenth state to adopt this nonpartisan approach.[15] In addition, to ensure unbiased results, strong regulations would be essential.

Therefore, another major objective of the Democracy Movement would be to have a redistricting commission in place for both state legislative districts and congressional districts by the commencement of the redistricting process following the 2020 census. If, due to the resistance of one party or the other, such a commission cannot be established by legislation, then the Democracy Movement should bypass the legislature of those states and put this issue on their election ballot prior to 2020. Since the populations of seven states are so small that they have only one congressional district, a redistricting commission would not be needed in those states.

Eliminating the Electoral College

The Democracy Movement should also demand the elimination of the Electoral College. If we are to have true political equity in the country, *every citizen's vote for president should carry the same weight.* After all, the president represents the people, not the states.

Since the Electoral College is a winner-take-all system in all but two states, citizens' votes in large states with more Electoral College votes are more important than those in small states. Thus a person's vote in California helps a candidate win fifty-five votes in the Electoral College, whereas someone's vote in Wyoming would assist the candidate who wins that state to obtain only three votes in the Electoral College. In addition, voters in swing states carry more weight than those in other states. Since the great majority of states are fairly certain to support one party's candidate or the other, how voters vote in the eight to twelve swing states usually determines the results of the election. But the votes of the citizens in these states should, in all fairness, not have any more significance than the votes of other citizens.

Since the president represents all the people equally, each person's vote should have the same weight, regardless of one's state of residence.

Significantly, the Electoral College creates the possibility for the loser of the popular vote to win the presidency. This happened in the 2000 election when Al Gore beat George Bush by over 1 million popular votes but Bush won the presidency because he had the majority of Electoral College votes and the Supreme Court decided to halt a full recount of Florida's election results.[16] Without question, eliminating the Electoral College would make our country more democratic.[17]

Protecting Voters' Rights

The right to vote is at the heart of a democratic society. The Democracy Movement must therefore fight to protect voters' rights. To assure the integrity of our elections, the movement must demand the elimination of restrictive voter ID laws and support the implementation of universal voter registration and hand-counting of paper ballots. Over the last fifteen years or more, the far right has been working to restrict or deny people's right to vote as well as to prevent the counting of all the ballots. Two private concerns, Diebold Election Systems and Election Systems and Software (ESS)— both of which have strong ties to the Republican Party—provide the vast majority of voting machines and forbid public scrutiny of them.[18] Thus even though the integrity of recent elections has been called into question, the public has no way to determine whether tampering with the voting machines has occurred or affected the outcome of those elections.[19] We cannot allow this to continue.

These suggestions are not meant to be an exhaustive list of what the Democracy Movement must address, which should be decided by a national conference or equivalent mechanism. Nevertheless, all the demands would be in keeping with its primary goal of establishing a vibrant democracy free of the corrupting influence of Big Money, where everyone can participate fully and freely in the democratic process and where our policymakers are accountable to the people.

To achieve these reforms and revive our democracy, we all must step up and vigorously build the Democracy Movement.

CHAPTER NINE

The Way Forward

As a grassroots democracy movement grows,
we can work together nationwide
to break Big Money's grip on America.

The period from 2015 through the 2020 elections will be a critical time for reviving democracy in America. Given the results of the 2014 midterm elections, as well as the significant strain between President Obama and the Republican Congress, Washington is almost certain to remain gridlocked until after the 2016 elections and possibly much longer. Moreover, Big Money will still be playing a dominant role in controlling government policy when the new president and Congress take office in January 2017.

Therefore, at least until the 2020 elections, a defining issue for the nation will be: Can the American people come together, stand up to Big Money, eliminate the corrupting influence of money in politics, and build a truly representative democracy in the United States before Big Money has virtually total control of our country?

In chapter 8, it was noted that Americans favor reducing the effects of money in politics by a huge majority. Voters support a constitutional amendment to overturn the *Citizens United* decision that money is speech and corporations are people by 73 percent to 23 percent. Furthermore, both Democratic and Republican voters strongly back tough campaign finance laws to limit the influence of money in politics.[1] However, since our government is now largely controlled by Big Money there is practically no possibility that Congress would support a constitutional amendment overturning *Citizens United* or enact effective campaign finance legislation. Based on the current campaign system, with its heavy dependence on building relationships with big donors, it also seems unlikely that a new president would lead the charge to overturn the process that played an important role in his or her election.

President Obama, whose campaigns have had many Big Money donors, is a prime example. Though he expressed strong support for campaign finance reform, including a constitutional amendment to overturn *Citizens United,* he has failed to take effective action to remedy the nation's corrupt campaign finance system.[2] Consequently, we, the people, are the only ones left to take on Big Money and thereby gain control of our government and revive democracy in America.

Convincing the American People to Take On Big Money

To convince the American people to take on Big Money, the Democracy Movement must reach out to all Americans, including the tens of millions who have dropped out of the political process. A huge number of Americans have given up on the political process, seeing government as corrupted by Big Money and concluding that involvement in politics is a waste of their time and energy. Therefore, an important strategy of the Democracy Movement must be to persuade a good number of these Americans that their participation in the political process *will* make a transformative difference.

How can the emerging Democracy Movement persuade Americans that their active engagement in it will fundamentally change a political system controlled by the most powerful entities in the country? First, the Democracy Movement's message needs to vividly illustrate how Big Money's grip on government denies millions of hardworking Americans their fair share of our country's wealth. It also must convince citizens that breaking Big Money's grip will put more money in their pockets and improve their lives.

Second, to achieve these goals, the Democracy Movement needs to focus on its key concerns and avoid the potentially divisive causes advocated by various factions within the movement. Two core issues that can bring Americans of all political persuasions together are political equality—the extent to which citizens have an equal voice in elections and governmental policy making[3]—and the elimination of government corruption. Polls indicate that 67 percent of Americans, including two-thirds of rank-and-file Republicans and a majority of Tea Party members, support eliminating super PACs and overturning the *Citizens United* decision,[4] both of which would greatly reduce the influence of money in politics.

The political system's failure to address these primary matters has led to the issue that is most likely to both galvanize public opinion and draw in millions of alienated Americans: growing income inequality. Consequently, it is critical for the Democracy Movement to stress the relationship between income inequality and political inequality. Income inequality, a major concern of many Americans, leads directly to political inequality. Since Big Money controls Congress, low- and middle-income Americans can't make their voices heard in Washington. This issue should garner more support for the

Democracy Movement because US income inequality is at its greatest level since 1928 and has risen steadily beginning in the 1970s. The bottom 90 percent of the population—almost 300 million people—now receives less than 50 percent of the nation's income for the first time ever. In contrast, the top 1 percent of Americans received 22.5 percent of all pre-tax income in 2012.[5]

In a November 2014 *Wall Street Journal*/NBC News poll, those saying "the system is stacked against them" included 58 percent of Democrats, 51 percent of Republicans, 55 percent of whites, 60 percent of blacks, 53 percent of Hispanics, as well as majorities of every age and professional cluster.[6] Consequently, it is essential that the Democracy Movement demonstrate how Big Money's grip on government increases income inequality and makes it more and more difficult for most Americans to maintain a decent standard of living. Significantly, just prior to the 2014 midterm elections, the Brookings Institution gauged the public's mood, with the following results: more than five years after the official end of the Great Recession, most people are frustrated by the stagnation of wages and household incomes. They are angry at a political system that seems incapable of acting on the most important challenges facing the country.[7]

Further, according to an October 2014 NBC/*Wall Street Journal* poll, "only 12 percent [of Americans] approve of the job Congress is doing; 83 percent disapprove. Only 30 percent think their representative deserves to be reelected, even lower than in the wave elections [that is, elections in which one major political party wins substantially more races than the other] of 2010 (37 percent), 2006 (39 percent), and 1994 (39 percent)."[8] As people's dissatisfaction and anger increase, they will be motivated to join the Democracy Movement and take action to fix the corrupt system that is rigged against them.

We, the people, must dispense with our despair and helplessness, join together, and instill in ourselves and one another the revolutionary spirit needed to revive democracy.

Creating a Strategy for Breaking Big Money's Grip

It is essential that the Democracy Movement do everything in its power to make political equality and the elimination of Big Money's grip on government the defining issues of the 2016 elections. The 2016 election campaigns can draw a distinct political line between the vast majority of Americans who favor political equality and democracy on one side and the plutocrats and their allies who want Big Money to control our nation's future on the other side. Because Big Money will vigorously oppose the Democracy Movement's mission and fight to maintain its control over both major political parties, the Democracy Movement will need to create an aggressive, comprehensive strategy for pursuing its agenda. Three essential elements of such a strategy are organization, education and training, and mobilization.

Organization

The Democracy Movement will require some degree of central leadership best implemented by a coordinating committee. The main functions of a Democratic Movement Coordinating Committee (DMCC) and support staff would be to develop strategy, promote the movement's vision and goals, build the movement, create educational materials, coordinate activities, and fundraise for the movement. The DMCC would consist of key personnel from member organizations and other local leaders from around the country who represent a broad segment of the population since the Democracy Movement needs to actively recruit groups and individuals from the entire political spectrum and demonstrate to them the value of joining the movement. Otherwise, political equality could become just another polarizing issue that would hamper the movement's ability to revive democracy in America.

While a coordinating committee is important in building a unified effort, the lifeblood of the Democracy Movement would be local Democracy Organizing Committees, or DOCs—an appropriate acronym for those working to revive our ailing political system—in towns and cities across the nation. In fact, it is quite likely that local DOCs could arise organically in communities around the country independent of any national Democracy Movement Coordinating Committee. Because Americans everywhere are angry and frustrated, they may naturally come together to address some of their concerns before any national DMCC is formed.

Here's where you come in. Aware of the increasing danger of Big Money's grip on our government, you can be the trailblazer who warns your community of the situation and begins to organize a local DOC. Like Paul Revere riding through the Massachusetts countryside alerting colonists at the beginning of the American Revolution that the "British are coming,"[9] today people are needed to sound the alarm that Big Money and corporate America are taking over our country. It is crucial that we all step up now, organize local DOCs, and work on reviving democracy in America before it is too late.

While the goal is not to take up arms against Big Money and corporate America, the objective is, in effect, to begin a second American Revolution. Prior to the first American Revolution, the colonists formed local "committees of correspondence" to rally opposition to Great Britain's unjust control over the colonies and establish plans for collective action.[10] Today, developing DOCs throughout the country is just as essential in furthering our cause.

Likewise, a DMCC may be formed by some of the national organizations working on reviving democracy. Once established, it would reach out to local affiliates of its member organizations to recruit volunteers seeking to organize local DOCs. Whether DOCs are initiated by a DMCC or arise organically in communities, they should be nonpartisan and diverse, including representatives of business, civic organizations, education, government, labor, minorities, and religious groups. To increase the chances for success the DOCs, unlike the Democracy Initiative and some other groups currently working to revive democracy in America, would reach out to organizations not associated with the Left or the Democratic Party, and include community leaders who might be more conservative or Republican. Organizations like the Chamber of Commerce, the Rotary Club, the League of Women Voters, and various church groups could provide more conservative DOC members and make committees more balanced and representative of the overall population. Ideally, a DOC would consist of fifteen to twenty-five community leaders and organizers.

The main roles of the local DOCs would be educating the people in their communities, organizing volunteers, advancing the movement's agenda, recruiting candidates to run for state and federal offices, and campaigning for Democracy Movement candidates. Local DOC membership would be decided on the basis of one's commitment to reviving democracy without regard to party politics. Participants would not be active members of a political party because this could represent a conflict of interest. Rather, committee members would be civic-minded individuals whose primary political concerns were eliminating the corrupting influence of money in politics, developing political equity so every citizen has an equal voice, and creating a political process in which our policymakers are accountable to the people and the public interest. A national network of local DOCs would create a truly grassroots Democracy Movement to revive our democracy by engaging millions of Americans in participatory government.

The time is ripe for organizing DOCs to campaign for the election of new congressional representatives and senators committed to breaking Big Money's grip on our government and reviving democracy in America.

Education and Training

Once the Democracy Movement puts out a "Call to Revive Democracy in America," the Movement would begin implementing an extensive education campaign across the country. It would need to develop clear, simple, and convincing educational materials highlighting how our government is controlled by Big Money, the detrimental effects this has on most Americans, and the significant benefits to the public in eliminating Big Money's grip. For example, the campaign could demonstrate how the American public is paying dearly while Big Money reaps huge rewards from corporate welfare, tax subsidies, and other business-friendly government programs and regulations. As noted in chapter 2, estimates are that the government provides corporate America with $100 billion or more a year in subsidies and tax breaks.[11] If Big Money's grip on government were broken, those subsidies and tax breaks could be eliminated and the resulting savings used in a myriad of useful ways to benefit average Americans such as providing incentives for small business development, increasing child care credits for working parents, improving our educational system, and repairing our infrastructure.

Important tools that the DOCs might use to educate, recruit, and organize people in their communities would be petition drives and voter pledges to hold our elected officials accountable. For instance, the DMCC could draft a petition calling for the elimination of the corrupting influence of money in politics and the establishment of a government that works for all the people of the United States. To achieve that, the petition would demand the implementation of the six goals stated in chapter 8.

Democracy Movement DOCs in every congressional district in the country could then circulate the petition to gather the signatures of hundreds of thousands—in some states, millions—of voters pledging to support only candidates who back the goals of the movement. Moreover, these voter pledges would indicate that if the elected officials do not deliver on their promises to work toward enacting the movement's goals then the voters would actively campaign to defeat the officials, regardless of party affiliation, in the next election and replace them with candidates committed to the movement's goals. It is essential that we have a clear and convincing mechanism, such as voter pledges, to hold our elected officials accountable.

After the local DOCs are formed and begin organizing in their communities, each state might convene a statewide Democracy Movement conference in the winter or early spring of 2016. All members of the local DOCs, as well as other local organizers, would be encouraged to attend. Each state conference might elect a statewide DOC Coordinating Committee. While DOC members would hopefully have some experience in political organizing, the conference would train them in promoting the movement's goals, organizing volunteers, conducting petition drives, developing town hall meetings, recruiting candidates for office, fundraising, working on campaigns, and other related matters. For people who could not attend the conference, online training could be provided.

At the state conferences, a Democracy Movement platform that included a mission and goals similar to those outlined in chapter 8 would be discussed and adopted. In addition, the conferences could organize local "Town Hall Meetings to Revive Democracy in America" to be held in the spring or early summer of 2016, ideally on the same day in hundreds of communities across the country. Once those attending the conferences return to their home communities, the DOCs would continue their local education efforts and petition drives, identify Democracy Movement–friendly candidates, and prepare for a town hall meeting in their communities.

A national conference in Washington, DC, might also be planned for late winter or early spring of 2016, providing the opportunity for movement leaders from around the country to meet and develop strategy for the 2016 fall election campaign. On the final day of the national conference, attendees could meet with their representatives and senators on Capitol Hill to inform them of the Democracy Movement's platform, as well as lobby them for their support of the movement's goals. In addition, the elected officials could be asked to sign a pledge committing to work and vote for the movement's six-point program.

Mobilization

As local DOCs are formed, they would begin identifying Democracy Movement–friendly candidates for state legislative office and Congress. Meetings would be held with potential candidates and legislators, or their staffs, to inform them of the Democracy Movement and gauge their support for the movement's goals. If a local DOC determines that a legislator did not strongly support the movement's goals, it would begin searching for a potential candidate who would challenge that legislator in the 2016 election and back the movement's goals. In addition to identifying a good challenger, such a search would be important for several reasons, including demonstrating to potential candidates that there is a growing movement for democratic change, cultivating potential candidates for future elections even if they were not ready to run in 2016, and finding candidates willing to make political equality and government corruption key election issues even if they did not have a very good chance of winning.

In late spring or early summer of 2016, a "National Town Hall Meeting to Revive Democracy in America" would be held on the same day in hundreds of locales across the country to spread the movement's message, inspire people to participate, and demonstrate national solidarity. Participants would be motivated to recruit more volunteers, as well as lobby candidates to pledge to support the Democracy Movement platform and, if elected, work for its enactment. The "National Town Hall Meeting to Revive Democracy in America" would provide a momentous opportunity to show the strength of the Democracy Movement. If hundreds of thousands, even millions, of people attended a multitude of town hall meetings around the country on the same day, the America. people would make a powerful statement calling for political equality for all and the elimination of Big Money's grip on our government.

Following their local town hall meetings, participants would meet with candidates running for the House of Representatives and Senate, as well as those running for state legislatures in the 2016 elections. At these meetings Democracy Movement activists would present the signed petitions of voters pledging to back candidates who support the movement's goals and urge their congressional representatives, as well as candidates for state and federal office, to pledge to actively support and vote for the legislative measures required to achieve these goals. If officials or candidates pledged to support the movement's platform, then the Democracy Movement would enthusiastically work to elect them.

During the summer and fall of 2016 prior to the elections, Democracy Movement activists would attend campaign events to question candidates regarding their positions on the movement's platform. At the same time, the Democracy Movement would continue its educational efforts to raise the public's awareness of the issues regarding political equity and government corruption, increase its ranks, and alert voters to the candidates' positions on the movement's goals.

In preparation for the 2016 presidential and congressional elections, Democracy Movement volunteers would also need to shadow both the presidential and congressional candidates from all parties and monitor their views during the primary season as well as the general election campaign. At every opportunity candidates should be asked to address the movement's goals and pledge their strong support for them. The local DOCs would be responsible for publicizing where each candidate stands on the movement's goals and whether candidates have pledged to work for enacting those goals if elected. Only through amassing tremendous numbers of citizens committed to the Democracy Movement will we be able to hold politicians to their promises.

The Democracy Movement's Role in 2017 and Beyond

While it is doubtful that the Democracy Movement can break Big Money's grip on our government in one election cycle, its efforts during the 2016 campaign can make a significant impact by:

- Building greater public support for political equality and the elimination of government corruption
- Increasing voter turnout
- Increasing the number of elected officials who make political equity and the elimination of government corruption priorities in their legislative agendas
- Setting the stage for a bigger, more effective campaign to break Big Money's grip in the 2018 election cycle.

People rising up during future election cycles in unprecedented numbers all over our country demanding an end to political corruption and requiring politicians to truly serve the American people would send a compelling message that politicians could not ignore. Those who dared to disregard the will of the people would be targeted for defeat. If the Democracy Movement determines over the next few years that it cannot achieve its goals by lobbying the existing parties and electing supportive representatives from them, then it should explore whether it has the strength to form a third political party, perhaps named the American People's Party, that could compete with the two existing dominant parties. While third parties in the United States have not fared well in the past, it may be the right moment for the emergence of a viable, new political party given the critical nature and urgency of the potential loss of democracy in our nation.

While Americans' growing anger and frustration at our unjust, plutocratic system is finally provoking us to action, perhaps more than anything else we need to reclaim our self-worth as an egalitarian people. We must believe that together we can break Big Money's grip so that, as Lincoln pleaded, "government of the people, by the people, for the people, shall not perish from the Earth."

CHAPTER TEN

We Are the Ones
We've Been Waiting For

*Every American who cares
about the future of this country
is at a moral and spiritual crossroads.*

B ig Money's grip on our political system is growing tighter and stifling democracy in America. If we are serious about pulling the country back from the brink of plutocracy and building a truly representative democracy in America, then we have to take action now. No one is going to do it for us, not Jeb Bush, Ben Carson, Hillary Clinton, Marco Rubio, Bernie Sanders, Donald Trump, Elizabeth Warren, or anyone else. It is up to us, the American people. We are the ones we've been waiting for.

In 1932, the nation was in the midst of the Great Depression. Millions of Americans had lost their jobs. Newly elected President Franklin D. Roosevelt met with labor leaders regarding policy initiatives they wanted the president to undertake to assist the ailing American workforce. At the conclusion of the meeting, Roosevelt allegedly stated, "I agree with you. I want to do it, now make me do it."[1] In effect, Roosevelt was telling the labor leaders that change had to come from the bottom up, not just from the White House. The president was saying that he needed the American people to continue pressing for the changes they wanted so he could have the strong backing required to ensure their enactment.[2] Similarly, today we all have an essential role in creating the government policies we desire by demanding fundamental changes in our political system.

Perhaps the American people did not take on this responsibility nearly as well as they could have when Barack Obama was elected in 2008. During his campaign for president, Obama promised "change you can believe in." However, the Obama administration did not make a serious effort to break Big Money's grip on our government. In fact, during Obama's presidency Big Money's grip has tightened and the country has moved closer to a full-blown plutocracy.

But as Roosevelt demanded of the labor leaders, did we press Obama (or Congress) to make him do it? If we want to revive democracy in America, we, the people, have to forcefully and continually battle for the necessary reforms.

Summoning the Courage to Fight for Democracy in America

Despite major obstacles, some Americans still have hope that our political system can be made to work for all of us, not just the wealthy and connected. We maintain faith that together we can progress toward achieving political equality and economic fairness. However, it will be necessary to devote substantial time, energy, and resources to accomplish this goal. The challenge subsequently becomes: are we willing, and do we have the courage, to join with millions of other Americans and fight to revive democracy in America?

To meet this challenge we may need to do some soul searching by asking ourselves the following questions:

- Do I want to live in a country where one out of every five children lives in poverty?[3]
- Do I want to live in a country where citizens' tax dollars support bailouts for reckless Wall Street ventures, corporate welfare, and government programs for millions of workers whose bosses won't pay them a living wage?
- Do I want to live in a country where Congress members' votes are bought by their Big Money sponsors in a corrupt system that disregards the public interest?
- Do I want to live in a nation where I am a second-class citizen with practically no voice in how my country is run?

Hopefully, many of us will say no to these questions. Then we will call on our friends and neighbors to join us in forming the Democracy Movement to take control of our country away from Big Money and put it in the people's hands. And we will do it because, just as in the days of the American Revolution, a higher authority is calling us and we know it is the right thing to do.

Using Strategies of the Underdog

We, the people, are clearly the underdog in our struggle against Big Money to revive democracy. A central factor in overcoming the mighty is to not play by their rules.[4] According to a study of two hundred years of war, when underdogs choose not to play by the rules of their powerful opponents they win "even when everything we think we know about power says they shouldn't."[5] And researchers have found that when underdogs acknowledge personal weaknesses, choose an unconventional strategy, and attack opponents' flaws or vulnerabilities they win over 60 percent of the battles.[6]

As children, most of us learned the biblical story of David and Goliath, in which the pint-sized David brought down the giant Goliath. Instead of using conventional weapons of battle, like a shield and sword, which even then would have rendered him no match to Goliath's skills, David used a mere slingshot and stones to kill his opponent. Moreover, David struck Goliath at one of his weakest points, his forehead, where there was an opening in the giant's armor.[7]

A more recent example of the underdog using an unconventional strategy and attacking its stronger opponent's weak spot is Lawrence of Arabia's assault on the Port of Aqaba near the end of World War I. Lawrence commanded a few hundred nomads against the modern Turkish army then occupying the port. While the Turks expected an attack from the sea, Lawrence and his band of Bedouins advanced on the city from the unprotected desert east of Aqaba. This unconventional plan, requiring a six-hundred-mile trek through the desert during the summer, was so daring that the Turks never saw it coming.[8]

The "weakness" of we, the people, the underdog in the current struggle to revive democracy, is the lack of funding to fill the airwaves, lobby politicians, and win elections. Big Money and corporate America's "flaws" are its corrupted values rooted in self-interest and the belief that the ends justify the means—values that resulted in the deceptive practices that brought about the 2008 Great Recession. If Big Money lived by the people's values of honesty, hard work, and fairness, perhaps the Great Recession would never have happened. Certainly, the vast majority of Americans would be better off today if corporate America viewed itself as a committed partner in the strengthening of a democratic American society and, consequently, placed a higher value on the public interest, or common good.

To win the struggle to revive democracy, we must expose Big Money's flawed values and demonstrate how playing by its rules is ruining the country and harming all its citizens.

The use of unconventional strategies to win against powerful political and social opponents is reflected in many historical events. In chapter 1, we noted how Rosa Parks used her unconventional strategy of refusing to move to the back of the bus to fight the powerful forces of segregation in Alabama. Likewise, Mahatma Gandhi implemented an unusual strategy in India—a nonviolent, 240-mile walk to the sea—to protest the British Empire's ban on Indians collecting or selling salt.[9] Being the underdog did not prevent the Indian people from standing up, fighting for their rights, and eventually winning.

Likewise, the Democracy Movement could develop unconventional strategies in its struggle to revive democracy in America. For example, in contrast to the conventional strategy of spending millions of dollars and flooding the airwaves with messages to convince people to support its mission, the Democracy Movement could use the Internet and face-to-face meetings to promote the movement's ideas. An even more unconventional strategy would be for the Democracy Movement to bridge the Republican-Democratic, conservative-liberal divide and find common ground for reviving democracy in America in contrast to the usual partisan approach to political issues.

Another tactic employed to gain victory over a more powerful opponent is the use of relentless effort to make up for any deficit in power or ability. In a *New Yorker* article, Malcolm Gladwell explains how this tactic has been used by a number of weak basketball teams to beat formidable opponents. By utilizing a full-court press (an aggressive defense involving all the players), these teams accomplished great feats, including winning national championships.[10] Similarly, the tireless effort of the American people in organizing and mobilizing the Democracy Movement can break Big Money's grip and help gain control of government.

Yet another tactic of the underdog in challenging powerful opposition is to possess moral authority, especially in connection with advantageous timing. It has been almost 240 years since our Founding Fathers stood up to the mighty British Empire and declared their right to self-governance. Those brave souls proclaimed in the Declaration of Independence that governments derive "their just powers from the consent of the governed." Though the odds were against them, they knew in their hearts it was the right thing to do, that their actions had moral authority.

Today, the odds are against us as well. Big Money and corporate America are powerful. But history has shown that regardless of the overwhelming strength of the opposition, standing up for what is just often yields surprisingly positive results. From such efforts as our own American Revolution, India's fight for independence from Great Britain, and the struggle of blacks to end Apartheid in South Africa, we know that right can win over might. Moreover, the Democracy Movement for political equality is imbued with a spiritual force; in our hearts we know that money and power are not the values that lie at the core of our beings or the essence of our society. People have been fighting for self-governance for centuries; an American democracy movement in the twenty-first century is therefore on the right side of history.

An American democracy movement is the moral imperative of our time.

Americans Working Together to Revive Democracy

Americans are blessed with a communal spirit. We often find a way, despite our differences, to come together and make circumstances better for everyone. Sadly, money and power have come to dominate our national narrative, while fairness, equality, and the common good have received far too little consideration.

Consequently, many of us are disheartened, perhaps angry or even outraged, by Big Money's grip on our government. We see the loss and suffering of millions of people, both here and abroad, due to the corruption, greed, and self-interest in our nation and, as individuals, we feel helpless to confront such overwhelming issues. But we are not alone. We can come together and collectively break Big Money's grip and fix our failed political system. Once we understand that practically 80 percent of Americans think our political system is corrupt and broken, and that an overwhelming majority of Americans favor aggressive measures to stem the corrupting influence of money in politics, we, the people—over 300 million strong—can work together to revive democracy.[11]

Just as the colonists did prior to the American Revolution, it is time for us to stand up and cry out, "Enough." We can rise above any differences we may have for the sake of our country, a better life for most Americans, and increased justice. When the United States was attacked at Pearl Harbor, Americans came together to fight a common enemy. Now the assault on our government is from within, but it is no less dangerous. By joining together in a national unity movement, we can rid the country of the destructive, overbearing plutocracy that is crushing the American Dream.

In fact, the American people are rising up and their voices are being heard. Millions in New York, as well as around the globe, marched in September 2014 demanding solutions to climate change.[12] Fast-food and other low-wage workers are organizing for a living wage. Protesters are attending bank shareholders meetings and insisting on real financial reform.[13] YouTube videoing, e-publishing, web conferencing, and other Internet tools are providing people with the means to raise their voices and spread their messages quickly and easily. The Democracy Movement can utilize these and other strategies to educate people, bring them together, and implement a plan to break Big Money's grip on government.

Unfortunately, Americans in lower- and middle-income brackets who are struggling just to get by may not have the time or resources to organize this cause. Therefore, those who have time, some expendable resources, and experience or talent could help facilitate the development of the Democracy Movement.

Many people who are stepping forward, myself included, are products of the 1960s. We were exhilarated by being called by a young president, John F. Kennedy, to "ask not what your country can do for you; ask what you can do for your country."[14] And we were dispirited when our hopes and dreams were repeatedly dashed by assassins' bullets and a senseless war on the other side of the globe. Still, we remain steadfast in our vision for a better tomorrow.

Now is the time to renew our dreams and pass them on to the next generation.

America at a Crossroads

The United States is at a moral and spiritual crossroads. It may even be fair to call it a crossroads comparable to the one before the Civil War. Then the issue that divided the nation was slavery versus freedom for all. Now it's plutocracy versus democracy.

Throughout our history, Americans have struggled to find some balance between capitalism and democracy. At other times, our political system more successfully kept our free enterprise economy somewhat managed or regulated. But now capitalism and democracy are clashing head on. At this point, the economic system controlled by Big Money and corporate America is overtaking our government, resulting in plutocracy, government by and for the wealthy. Rather than having an economic order that fosters democracy, unbound capitalism in the United States has become a "constant threat to the egalitarianism and popular rule that democracy stands for."[15]

Are we going to say it's hopeless and allow democracy, the heart and soul of America, to die? Are we going to leave to our children and grandchildren a country controlled by a corrupt political system that has no allegiance to government by and for the people and no concern for the common good? Or are we going to stand up to Big Money and corporate America and fight to revive democracy and our right to self-governance?

The founders of our nation signed the Declaration of Independence willing to die, if necessary, to gain freedom from the British Empire, stating that "with a firm reliance on the protection of divine Providence, we mutually pledge to each other our Lives, our Fortunes and our sacred Honor." Since then millions of Americans have sacrificed their lives valiantly fighting for freedom and justice. While today the forces opposing our democratic way of life are neither foreign nor military, they are as strong and dangerous as America has ever faced in the past.

Now it is our turn to answer the call to revive democracy in America. We are the ones we've been waiting for.

Afterword

A democracy movement to break Big Money's grip on our government is only going to happen if we, the people, make it happen. Building a mass movement that involves millions of people from across the political spectrum and helps transform our government into one that truly serves the American people requires a strong commitment from each of us. If we are going to revive our democracy, we will need to roll up our sleeves and dig into our pockets.

I hope you'll be willing to help build the Democracy Movement. If you agree with the basic ideas in *Breaking Big Money's Grip on America,* I encourage you to share this book with family, friends, and colleagues with diverse political views; talk about these issues; and consider establishing a Democracy Organizing Committee (DOC) in your town or city, county, or state. I would be interested in learning about your experiences as you begin working on reviving democracy in America. To share your insights and observations, please visit the blog Revivingdemocracy.org. You can also go to the website breakingbigmoneysgrip.com for more information.

The Democracy Movement needs all of us—now.

Appendix

The following is a partial list of national organizations, some with local affiliates, that are working to revive democracy in America in various ways, along with their websites. If you contact any of them, please feel free to mention *Breaking Big Money's Grip on America* and to encourage the organization to become part of the Democracy Movement.

Center for Responsive Politics—www.publicintegrity.org
Common Cause—www.commoncause.org
The Democracy Initiative—www.democracyforus.org
Democracy Matters—www.democracymatters.org
Demos—www.demos.org
End Citizens United—www.endcitizensunited.org
Free Speech for People—www.freespeechforpeople.org
Inequality For All—www.inequalityforall.com
Issue One—www.issueone.org
League of Women Voters—www.lwv.org
Liberty Tree Foundation—www.LibertyTreeFoundation.org
Mayday PAC—www.Mayday.us
Move to Amend—www.movetoamend.org
National Election Integrity Coalition—www.democracymovement.us
Move On—www.MoveOn.org
People for the American Way—www.pfaw.org
Populist 2015 Alliance—www.populism2015.org
Public Campaign—www.publiccampaign.org
Public Citizen—www.citizen.org
Reclaim Democracy—www.reclaimdemocracy.org
Represent.us—www.represent.us
Rootstrikers—www.Rootstrikers.org
Rotary Club—www.rotary.org
The Stamp Stampede—www.stampstampede.org
Take Back Our Republic—www.takeback.org
Wolf-PAC—www.wolf-pac.com

Notes

Chapter 1

1. http://bit.ly/1aVqQ5A.
2. Patrick Caddell, et al., "Americans Consensus: Fix the Corrupt System," PopularResistanceOrg, July 5, 2014, http://bit.ly/1zNKGX1.
3. http://bit.ly/1Kz7AHF.
4. http://bit.ly/1OfKZWw.
5. http://bit.ly/1bFJewr.
6. "Don't Let Big Oil Rig the Debate," http://bit.ly/1DPX3pl.
7. Richard, Schiffman, "Evil Monsanto Aggressively Sues Farmers for Saving Seeds," Alternet, http://bit.ly/1K6wAWC.
8. http:www.npc.umich.edu/poverty/.
9. http://1.usa.gov/1gpivYT.
10. "Rosa Louise McCauley Parks," Montgomery Bus Boycott RSS, http://bit.ly/1DPXUGr.

Chapter 2

1. http://bit.ly/1wFKsT1.
2. "Senator Warren Calls On House to Strike Repeal of Dodd-Frank Provision from Government Spending Bill," December 10, 2014, http://1.usa.gov/1dlvJGY.
3. Mary Bottari, "Congress to Reinstate Taxpayer Subsidies for Reckless Derivatives Trading," *Common Dreams*, December 11, 2014, http://bit.ly/1bLXBDE.
4. http://en.wikipedia.org/wiki/Troubled_Asset_Relief_Program.
5. http://whttp://postcalc.usps.gov/ww.sourcewatch.org/index.php/Portal:-Real_Economy_Project.
6. Mary Bottari, Rebecca Shabad, et al., "Senate Passes $1.2T Funding Bill," December 13, 2014, http://bit.ly/1uEHCto; and "Congress to Reinstate Taxpayer Subsidies for Reckless Derivatives Trading," *Truth-Out*, http://bit.ly/1EKfShn.
7. Drew Desilver, "Making More Than Minimum Wage, but Less Than $10.10 an Hour," Pew Research Center RSS, November 5, 2014, http://pewrsr.ch/1OwyNAB.
8. Ali Meyer, "1 in 5 Children Live in Poverty in U.S.," June 3, 2014, http://bit.ly/1A79UQl.

9. http://on.wsj.com/IDuliQ.

10. Kenneth Vogel, "Budget Rider Would Expand Party Cash," *POLITICO*, December 10, 2014, http://politi.co/1qt26Jb.

11. http://ourfuture.org/20150327/now-we-know-why-huge-tpp-trade-deal-is-kept-secret-from-the-public.

12. Bill Quigley, "Ten Examples of Welfare for the Rich and Corporations," *The Huffington Post*, January 14, 2014, http://huff.to/LwZLtw.

13. Robert Pear, "Bill to Let Medicare Negotiate Drug Prices Is Blocked," *New York Times*, April 17, 2007, http://nyti.ms/1QBDSpO.

14. Peter Baker, "Obama Was Pushed by Drug Industry, E-Mails Suggest," *New York Times*, June 8, 2012, http://nyti.ms/1aEyi4Z.

15. Jon Reynolds, "The Screeching Kettle: Both Republicans and Democrats Are Whores for Big Pharma," January 2, 2014, http://bit.ly/1bpLc7C.

16. http://bit.ly/1db8gA2.

17. http://bit.ly/1FkM2Pa, http://bit.ly/1aZfqhd.

18. http://bit.ly/1OZ9iTy.

19. Brad Johnson, "Poll: 74 Percent of Americans Favor Ending Big Oil Subsidies," March 3, 2011, http://bit.ly/1z38Cuj.

20. "Scientific Opinion on Climate Change," Wikipedia, http://bit.ly/1HIqsV0.

21. Tom Murse, "Global Warming Hoax—5 Members of Congress Who Don't Believe in Climate Change," http://abt.cm/1zaRe7k.

22. Alan Berlow, et al., "Gun Lobby's Money and Power Still Holds Sway over Congress," Center for Public Integrity, May 1, 2013, http://bit.ly/1EGKErf.

23. Michael Planty, et al., Bureau of Justice Statistics, May 7, 2013, http://1.usa.gov/1v9wpjV.

24. "Release Detail," Quinnipiac University, July 3, 2014, http://bit.ly/1pLfQhA.

25. Alan Berlow, et al., "Gun Lobby's Money and Power."

26. Ibid.

27. Bruce Watson, "The 10 Biggest Corporate Campaign Contributors in U.S. Politics," *DailyFinance* (DailyFinance.com), October 14, 2010, http://aol.it/1EuEVTo.

28. "Defense," Opensecrets RSS, http://bit.ly/1FoVhhk.

29. Donny Shaw, "The Campaign Contributions Behind the World's Most Expensive Weapon," July 22, 2014, http://maplight.org/content/73500; and "Granger, Dicks Announce Congressional Joint Strike Fighter Caucus," November 9, 2011, http://1.usa.gov/1zaVljD.

30. Ben Freeman, "Buying the Joint Strike Fighter Caucus," Opensecrets RSS, December 14, 2011, http://bit.ly/1OVOGf1.

31. Winslow Wheeler, "How the F-35 Nearly Doubled in Price (And Why You Didn't Know)," July 9, 2012, http://ti.me/1JtEwDW; and Hayes Brown, "Americans Have Spent Enough Money on a Broken Plane to Buy Every Homeless Person a Mansion," ThinkProgress RSS, July 9, 2014, http://bit.ly/1oIikK5.

32. Ellen Hodgson Brown, *The Web of Debt: The Shocking Truth about Our Money System and How We Can Break Free,* 5th ed. (Baton Rouge, LA: Third Millennium Press, 2012), 101.

33. Ketchum, Richard, *Divided Loyalties: How the American Revolution Came to New York* (New York: Henry Holt and Company, 2002); and Harlow Unger, *John Hancock: Merchant King and American Patriot* (New York: John Wiley & Sons, 2000).

34. David Korten, *When Corporations Rule the World* (Bloomfield, CT: Kumarian Press, 1995).

35. Matthew Josephson, *The Robber Barons* (New York: Mariner Books, 1962).

36. http://bit.ly/1DBhPpo.

37. http://bit.ly/1JIAO62.47.

Chapter 3

1. http://www.thisdayinquotes.com/2010/01/business-of-america-is-business.html.

2. Drew Desilver, "U.S. Income Inequality, on Rise for Decades, Is Now Highest Since 1928," Pew Research Center RSS, December 5, 2013, http://pewrsr.ch/18oh9Fz.

3. http://on.wsj.com/IDuliQ.

4. Louis Efron, "Creating Life Balance to Achieve Success," *Forbes* (August 28, 2014), http://onforb.es/1rBZfOe; and William Torbert, *The Power of Balance: Transforming Self, Society, and Scientific Inquiry* (Newbury Park, CA: Sage, 1991).

5. Jeanane Fowler, *Humanism: Beliefs and Practices* (Portland, OR: Sussex Academic Press, 1999), 140.

6. http://en.wikipedia.org/wiki/Middle_Way.

7. http://teaminfocus.com.au/the-virtue-of-balance/.

8. https://prezi.com/luq_n3h724bg/a-balanced-society/.

9. Sam Stein, "Obama Has Met at Least 27 Times with Private Health Care Industry Executives," *The Huffington Post*, August 22, 2009, http://huff.to/1FUbv0n.

10. http://on.wsj.com/1FCNCHA. http://huff.to/1ILy22T.

11. http://bit.ly/1H8EBL1.

12. http://huff.to/1AhKgfr.

13. Ibid.

14. http://bit.ly/1FLDVac.

15. http://nyti.ms/1POHhkL http://nyti.ms/1DIKTQj.

16. http://articles.latimes.com/2001/aug/26/news/mn-38530.

17. http://bit.ly/1FLIYr0.

18. http://tvnewslies.org/html/powell_lies_to_un.html.

19. http://www.motherjones.com/politics/2011/12/leadup-iraq-war-timeline; and http://www.digitalnpq.org/articles/global/30/10-28-2005/scott_ritter.

20. http://nyti.ms/1HulCLj.

21. http://www.motherjones.com/politics/2011/12/leadup-iraq-war-timeline.

22. http://bit.ly/1frRDHr.

23. http://bit.ly/1FUmW84.

24. http://bit.ly/1aWpSWX. http://reut.rs/1zhDbap. http://bit.ly/1FTM4yK; and http://bit.ly/1ro9ANy. http://bit.ly/1bjmNw3.

25. http://bit.ly/1H8R4y8.

26. http://fxn.ws/1zhFXfX. http://aol.it/1b43dsp.

27. David Daycn, "Barney Frank's Biggest Bombshell: His Shocking Anecdote about the Financial Crisis," Alternet, March 31, 2015, http://bit.ly/1b43RX2.

28. http://bit.ly/1CLA7ov.

29. http://bit.ly/1CLADmu.

30. Ibid.

31. Dayen, "Barney Frank's Biggest Bombshell."

32. "Obama Signs Monsanto Protection Act! Betrays America," March 27, 2013, http://bit.ly/1b7B2Il.

33. http://bit.ly/1CLFrZ4.

34. David Knowles, "Opponents of Genetically Modified Organisms in Food, or GMOs, Rail...," March 25, 2013, http://nydn.us/1aWGzS4.

35. http://bit.ly/1RT5GG0.

36. Holt, Steve, "Monsanto Protection Act Sneaks Through Senate," *TakePart*, March 22, 2013, http://bit.ly/1DJ5QdP.

Chapter 4

1. http://bit.ly/1G0pLY1.
2. http://ti.me/1b7GImz.
3. John F. Kennedy, "To Keep the Lobbyist within Bounds," *New York Times Magazine*, February 19, 1956; Congressional Record, March 2, 1956, 38023.
4. http://theatln.tc/1QaJpDI.
5. http://bit.ly/1CTvA2e.
6. http://bit.ly/1Da3wrF.
7. http://www.commoncause.org.
8. http://bit.ly/1fXrIGX; http://bit.ly/1IjnPHw;http://bit.ly/1Da3wrF.
9. "House's Author of Drug Benefit Joins Lobbyists," *New York Times,* December 16, 2004, 1.
10. Ibid.
11. Ibid.
12. http://bloom.bg/XORbvZ.
13. Mark Leibovich, *This Town* (London: Blue Rider Press, 2013), 330.
14. http://www.nytimes.com/2013/07/28/books/review/this-town-by-mark-leibovich.html?pagewanted=all&_r=0http://nyti.ms/1v7P6Xj.
15. www.gephardtDC.com.
16. www.Wikipedia.com/Evan Bayh.
17. http://huff.to/1OkcQ2x.
18. Eric Lipton, "Law Doesn't End Revolving Door on Capitol Hill," *New York Times,* February 1, 2014, http://nyti.ms/1cAjFkJ.
19. http://ti.me/1JNTvpE.
20. http://bit.ly/1jjbtR0.
21. http://theatln.tc/1b7h7tU.
22. http://bit.ly/1FY6eVv.
23. http://theatln.tc/1b7h7tU.
24. http://www.alec.org/model-legislation/.
25. http://www.alecexposed.org/wiki/What_is_ALEC%3F.
26. http://www.sourcewatch.org/index.php/ALEC_Corporations.
27. http://www.alecexposed.org/wiki/What_is_ALEC%3F.
28. Ibid.

29. http://bit.ly/1yz5cja.

30. http://www.sourcewatch.org/index.php/ALEC_Politicians#ALEC_
    Alumni_in_Congress.

Chapter 5

1. Buckley v. Valeo, 424 U.S. 1 (1976).

2. Citizens United v. Federal Election Commission, 558 U.S. 310 (2010).

3. George Orwell, *1984* (New York: Harcourt Brace Jovanovich, 1949).

4. http://en.wikipedia.org/wiki/Doublespeak.

5. McCutcheon v. Federal Election Commission, 572 U.S. ___ (2014).

6. Ibid.

7. http://www.washingtonpost.com/blogs/the-fix/wp/2014/03/25/shel-
   don-adelson-spent-93-million-on-the-2012-election-heres-how/.

8. http://bit.ly/1y4Nf6u; http://bit.ly/1CVhhvb.

9. http://politi.co/1nnUOU7.

10. http://wapo.st/1DbGVgg.

11. http://nyti.ms/1j8fsD3.

12. http://wapo.st/1DbGVgg.

13. http://bit.ly/1G4fo5M.

14. http://www.huffingtonpost.com/2014/03/11/campaign-donations-ac-
    cess_n_4941357.html.

15. Jeff Connaughton, *The Payoff: Why Wall Street Always Wins* (Westport,
    CT: Prospecta Press, 2012).

16. http://articles.courant.com/1998-04-29/news/9804290653_1_public-
    campaign-sen-christopher-j-dodd-campaign-finance-reform.

17. http://www.opensecrets.org/news/2013/09/mccutcheons-multiply-
    ing-effect-why/.

18. http://bit.ly/1DspbyD; http://bit.ly/1DQTXCA.

19. http://bit.ly/1HgOFS9.

20. http://wapo.st/1pxoqfd; http://ampr.gs/1GUHWi5.

Chapter 6

1. http://www.history.com/topics/labor.

2. http://www.historynet.com/abolitionist-movement. http://1.usa.
   gov/1ynH6Ex.

3. http://bit.ly/1gMhRko.

4. http://en.wikipedia.org/wiki/Civil_Rights_Act_of_1964; and http://en.wikipedia.org/wiki/Voting_Rights_Act_of_1965.

5. http://www.ushistory.org/us/55d.asp.

6. http://bit.ly/1E2K0Sz.

7. http://bit.ly/1cUznPG.

8. https://movetoamend.org.

9. https://represent.us.

10. https://mayday.us.

11. http://www.takeback.org/content/page/about.

Chapter 7

1. Caroline Fairchild, "Occupy Arrests Near 8,000 as Wall Street Eludes Prosecution," *The Huffington Post*, May 23, 2013, http://huff.to/1oSTp3K.

2. Michael Lewin, "Martin Luther King Jr.: The Civil Rights Movement and Gandhian Philosophy," The Gandhi Foundation, June 16, 2008, http://bit.ly/1EkSpTx.

3. https://www.gilderlehrman.org/history-by-era/age-reagan/time-line-terms/reagan's-"morning-america."

Chapter 8

1. "The Democracy Initiative," The Democracy Initiative, http://www.democracyforus.org.

2. http://bit.ly/1Fey8Ok.

3. http://bit.ly/1DjFjCw.

4. http://bit.ly/1IIkAtw.

5. http://bit.ly/1GmiRK5.

6. http://www.democracymovement.us.

7. http://bit.ly/1INktge.

8. "Public Campaign," *Campaign Finance Reform a Tea Party Issue*, June 20, 2014, http://bit.ly/1OzHWTR.

9. "An Idea Whose Time Has Come," www.democracycorps.com, July 31, 2014, http://bit.ly/1P6XnoJ.

10. Kenneth Vogel, "Fighting Big Donors with Big Dollars," *POLITICO*, February 11, 2014, http://politi.co/MUhGui.

11. Ibid.

12. Adam Serwer, et al., "Now That's What I Call Gerrymandering!" *Mother Jones*, November 14, 2012, http://bit.ly/1hhCrKR.

13. Sam Wang, "The Great Gerrymander of 2012," *New York Times*, February 2, 2013, http://nyti.ms/1cCeVHJ. http://bit.ly/1zumE2E.

14. "Ralph Nader on GOP," *Democracy Now!* November 6, 2014, http://bit.ly/1ss5Xl6.

15. Associated Press, "Redistricting Commission Approved by NY Voters," November 5, 2014, http://bit.ly/1K0fXfr.

16. Robert Longley, "Electoral College System: How to Lose, but Win an Election," http://abt.cm/1D7bstn; and https://en.wikipedia.org/wiki/Florida_election_recount.

17. Eric Black, "10 Reasons Why the Electoral College Is a Problem," *MinnPost*, October 16, 2012, http://bit.ly/190S33n.

18. Bob Fitrakis, et al., "Diebold's Political Machine," *Mother Jones*, March 5, 2004, http://bit.ly/1G1rtTK.

19. Bob Fitrakis, et al., "How the GOP Bought, Rigged, Stole and Lynched the 2014 Election," *Common Dreams,* November 11, 2014, http://bit.ly/1Ha8tIq.

Chapter 9

1. Stan Greenberg, et al., "An Idea Whose Time Has Come," www.democracycorps.com, July 31, 2014, http://bit.ly/1P6XnoJ; and Kenneth Vogel, "Fighting Big Donors with Big Dollars," *POLITICO*, February 11, 2014, http://politi.co/MUhGui.

2. Juliet Eilperin, "Obama's Campaign Finance Reform Plans Have Faded," April 29, 2013, http://wapo.st/1JJndvo.

3. http://bit.ly/1DdqYoM.

4. ABC News/*Washington Post* Poll, "Seven in 10 Would Send Super PACS Packing," March 13, 2012, http://bit.ly/1Km8Wpf.

5. Drew Desilver, "U.S. Income Inequality, on Rise for Decades, Is Now Highest Since 1928," Pew Research Center RSS, December 5, 2013, http://pewrsr.ch/18oh9Fz.

6. Neil King Jr., "Americans of All Stripes Agree: The System Is Stacked against Them," Washington Wire RSS, November 20, 2014, http://on.wsj.com/14QSJJx.

7. William Galston, "2014 Midterms: Voters Head to the Polls Frustrated and Angry at Congress, President," The Brookings Institution, October 27, 2014, http://brook.gs/1bv8gBU.

8. Ibid.

9. https://www.paulreverehouse.org/ride/real.html.

10. https://en.wikipedia.org/wiki/Committee_of_correspondence.

11. http://robertreich.org/post/119938747675.

Chapter 10

1. "Talk: Franklin D. Roosevelt," Wikiquote. http://bit.ly/1GbRTlS.

2. Tim Price, "Keeping Them Honest: What Politicians Say vs. What We Make Them Do," http://bit.ly/1IJKSf1.

3. Valerie Strauss, "New Census Data: Children Remain America's Poorest Citizens," *Washington Post,* September 17, 2013.

4. Malcolm Gladwell, "How David Beats Goliath—The New Yorker," *New Yorker,* May 11, 2009, http://nyr.kr/1mqH06U.

5. http://bit.ly/1eZ2731.

6. Gladwell, "How David Beats Goliath."

7. Malcolm Gladwell, *David and Goliath* (New York: Little, Brown and Company, 2013), 8.

8. Ibid.

9. http://www.history.com/topics/salt-march.

10. Patrick Caddell, et al., "Americans Consensus: Fix the Corrupt System," PopularResistanceOrg, July 5, 2014, http://bit.ly/1zNKGX1.

11. Zachary Roth, "Fighting Corruption Polls off the Charts," Msnbc.com, December 3, 2013, http://on.msnbc.com/1yU0A7c.

12. "How Many Steps Will You March?" http://climatemarch.org. 3; and Roger Hickey, "The New Populist Movement: Organizing to Take Back America," Campaign for America's Future, March 16, 2014, http://bit.ly/1DFine3.

14. http://voicesofdemocracy.umd.edu/kennedy-inaugural-address-speech-text/.

15. Chris Hedges, et al., "Can Capitalism and Democracy Coexist?" October 23, 2014, http://bit.ly/1DUOvNZ.

Bibliography

Alperovitz, Gar. *What Then Must We Do? Straight Talk about the Next American Revolution.* White River Junction, VT: Chelsea Green Publishing, 2013.

Brown, Ellen Hodgson. *Web of Debt: The Shocking Truth about Our Money System and How We Can Break Free, 5th ed.* Baton Rouge, LA: Third Millennium Press, 2012.

Connaughton, Jeff. *The Payoff: Why Wall Street Always Wins.* Westport, CT: Prospecta Press, 2012.

Fowler, Jeanane. *Humanism: Beliefs and Practices.* Portland, OR: Sussex Academic Press, 1999.

Hacker, Jacob S., and Paul Pierson. *Winner-Take-All Politics: How Washington Made the Rich Richer—and Turned Its Back on the Middle Class.* New York: Simon & Schuster, 2010.

Josephson, Matthew. *The Robber Barons.* New York: Mariner Books, 1962.

Ketchum, Richard. *Divided Loyalties: How the American Revolution Came to New York.* New York: Henry Holt and Company, 2002.

Korten, David C. *When Corporations Rule the World.* Bloomfield, CT: Kumarian Press, 1995.

Leibovich, Mark. *This Town: Two Parties and a Funeral — Plus Plenty of Valet Parking!* — in America's Gilded Capital. London: Blue Rider Press, 2013.

Lessig, Lawrence. *Republic, Lost: How Money Corrupts Congress and a Plan to Stop It.* New York: Twelve Books, 2011.

Orwell, George. *1984.* New York: Harcourt Brace Jovanovich, 1949.

Torbert, William. *The Power of Balance: Transforming Self, Society, and Scientific Inquiry.* Newbury Park, CA: Sage, 1991.

Unger, Harlow. *John Hancock: Merchant King and American Patriot.* New York: John Wiley & Sons, 2000.

Index

About the Author

A public sector attorney and social change activist, Bruce Berlin has devoted himself to social justice issues for over forty-five years. Berlin earned his AB in government from Cornell University and his JD from New York University. Following graduation from law school in 1970, he began his legal career assisting low-income clients at the Legal Aid Society in Trenton, New Jersey. A few years later he moved to Massachusetts and continued his poverty law practice with Western Massachusetts Legal Services. Prior to his retirement in the fall of 2012, he spent eight years as a senior attorney with the New Mexico Public Education Department, where he brought disciplinary charges against educators for violations of the department's Code of Ethics.

Before settling in Massachusetts, Berlin traveled abroad for a year, including studying Buddhism and practicing meditation under Lama Thubten Yeshe and Lama Thubten Zopa Rinpoche at Kopan, a Tibetan monastery in Nepal. Some years later he became a student of Zen meditation under Joshu Sasaki Roshi. Berlin is currently certified in Negotiation and Mediation by the National Center for Collaborative Planning and Community Services and in Economic Development by the New Mexico Community Economic Development Leadership Institute.

Berlin is the founder and former executive director of The Trinity Forum for International Security and Conflict Resolution, a nonprofit organization that brought together policymakers from a wide spectrum of political perspectives, professors of government and politics, NGO organizers, and concerned citizens to develop broad-based approaches to a variety of policy issues from national security in the nuclear age to economic development and diversification. While directing The Trinity Forum, Berlin was awarded a Jennings Randolph Peace Fellowship from the United States Institute of Peace in 1988. As a Peace Fellow, he studied the Nicaraguan conflict and produced a dialogue at the Armand Hammer United World College, which brought together high-level representatives of the Sandinista government and the Contras resistance movement, as well as US ambassadors to Central America, to explore paths to a Nicaraguan peace agreement.

During his career, Berlin has been involved in a number of local, state, and national political campaigns. In 1976, he helped direct a grassroots campaign for sheriff in Franklin County, Massachusetts. In the early 1980s, as a cofounder and state coordinator of the New Mexico Nuclear Freeze Campaign, he directed a successful statewide effort to lobby the New Mexico legislature for the passage of a resolution in support of a US-Soviet freeze on the development and deployment of nuclear weapons.

Formerly married, he has a daughter, Gioia, who is studying in Asia at the Global Studies Program of Long Island University. Berlin lives in Santa Fe, New Mexico, where, since 1981, he has worked on reviving democracy in America, promoting peace in the Middle East, and diversifying Los Alamos National Laboratory, among other issues. This is his first book.